bébé gourmet

100 French-Inspired Baby Food Recipes
for Raising an Adventurous Eater

Jenny Carenco

with contributions by Dr. Jean Lalau Keraly
photographs by Frédéric Lucano
translated from the French by Christine Buckley

THE EXPERIMENT
NEW YORK

BÉBÉ GOURMET: *100 French-Inspired Baby Food Recipes for Raising an Adventurous Eater*
Copyright © 2009, 2013 Jenny Carenco
Translation copyright © 2013 Christine Buckley
Photographs copyright © 2009 Frédéric Lucano

All rights reserved. Except for brief passages quoted in newspaper, magazine, radio, television, or online reviews, no portion of this book may be reproduced, distributed, or transmitted in any form or by any means, electronic or mechanical, including photocopying, recording, or information storage or retrieval system, without the prior written permission of the publisher.

The Experiment, LLC
260 Fifth Avenue
New York, NY 10001-6408
www.theexperimentpublishing.com

Bébé Gourmet was first published in 2009 by Marabout Editions as *Mon Livre des Recettes pour Bébé*. This revised and updated English-language edition is published by arrangement with Marabout.

The Experiment's books are available at special discounts when purchased in bulk for premiums and sales promotions as well as for fundraising or educational use. For details, contact us at info@theexperimentpublishing.com.

Many of the designations used by manufacturers and sellers to distinguish their products are claimed as trademarks. Where those designations appear in this book and The Experiment was aware of a trademark claim, the designations have been capitalized.

This book contains the opinions and ideas of its author. It is intended to provide helpful and informative material on the subjects addressed in the book. It is sold with the understanding that the author and publisher are not engaged in rendering medical, health, or any other kind of personal professional services in the book. The author and publisher specifically disclaim all responsibility for any liability, loss, or risk—personal or otherwise—that is incurred as a consequence, directly or indirectly, of the use and application of any of the contents of this book.

Library of Congress Cataloging-in-Publication Data

Carenco, Jenny.
  [Mon livre de recettes pour bébé. French]
  Bébé gourmet : 100 French-inspired baby food recipes for raising an adventurous eater / Jenny Carenco ; With the advice and support of Dr. Jean Lalau Keraly ; Photography by Frédéric Lucano ; Translated from French by Christine Buckley.
      pages cm
  ISBN 978-1-61519-070-6 (pbk.)—ISBN 978-1-61519-169-7 (ebook)
  1. Baby foods. 2. Infants—Nutrition. 3. Cooking, French. 4. Cookbooks. I. Keraly, Jean Lalau. II. Lucano, Fred, photographer. III. Buckley, Christine, 1972- translator. IV. Title.
  TX740.C28813 2013
  641.3'00832—dc23
                    2012038614

ISBN 978-1-61519-070-6
Ebook ISBN 978-1-61519-169-7

Cover design by Alison Forner and Lindsey Andrews
Cover photographs by Frédéric Lucano
Author photograph by Jean-Claude Amiel
Food styling by Sonia Lucano
Recipe testing by Alisa Morov
Text design by Marabout

Manufactured in China
Distributed by Workman Publishing Company, Inc.
Distributed simultaneously in Canada by Thomas Allen and Son Ltd.
First published April 2013

10 9 8 7 6 5 4 3 2 1

For Maya and Milo . . .

Contents

first compotes & first purées (4 months+)

first lunches & first sweets (6 months+)

first dinners (9 months+)

Author's Note

This is not the story of one of those perfect mothers who, for some reason the rest of us will never understand, manages to put a homemade meal on the table every night, including home-baked rolls that she prepares without ever breaking one of her perfectly manicured nails. This is *my* story, the story of your average Super Mom. She wants the best for her kids and, through trial and error, has found a way to cook tasty and nutritious meals for her baby—without quitting her job, reducing her nightly sleep to two hours, or hiring round-the-clock staff. This book is the fruit of my kitchen adventures; it is my personal notebook, the essence of my baby-feeding years, the results of my trials, the shortcuts and tricks that I found to make cooking for my kids a fun and relatively easy way to share my passion for good food and healthy eating.

My story starts six months after my daughter Maya was born. Introducing my little angel to her first foods had suddenly crawled its way to the top of my priority list, so I happily made my way down the baby food aisle of my favorite supermarket to choose what was going to be Maya's first experience with solid food. "Sweet peas" read one label. *Great*, I thought, *I love sweet peas and I know how nutritious and fiber-rich they are.* Yet, how strangely gray the purée looked. What was *really* in there? I took a closer look at the label. Water, starch, and just 22 percent sweet peas? And the labels went on like this—row after row, shelf after shelf, disappointment after disappointment. *This* is what we're feeding our kids in France, the country whose gastronomy made the United Nations World Heritage List? I was stunned. Needless to say, I left the supermarket empty-handed, and a little bit troubled, since I knew that (a) I was never going to feed Maya those "sweet peas" from the baby food aisle, (b) I was supposed to start working in five days, and (c) I had little-to-no knowledge about how to cook baby food myself.

The other half of my brain told me everything was going to be fine! I love cooking. Baby food might require a slightly different set of skills from pulling together dinner for my husband and myself, not to mention consideration of food sensitivities and avoiding potential allergies, but I had the strongest tool of all—motivation. *Sweet pea purée?* I can make that! *Beef stew for babies?* Hmm . . . I guess I can cook some up. *Baby-friendly fish casserole?* Okay, I would have to research that one, but it couldn't be impossible. I was determined to figure it all out when I got home, and even made a promise to Maya:

"Mom is going to cook yummy little dishes for you, and you're going to learn to love all the wonderful fruits, veggies, and other foods that your dad and I do. You're going to bite into life with curiosity and appetite; you're going to be healthy and happy. I want you to be an adventurous eater, my child!"

Later that night, when my family was sleeping, I started to study the art of cooking for my baby. It wasn't as complicated as I thought. Fears of food allergies, intolerances, choking, rashes, and the other scenarios I had drawn up in my head quickly vanished and I began to think up recipe ideas for Maya. We started with the basics: carrots, green beans, sweet peas, pumpkin, broccoli . . . and Maya loved them all! My husband and I like our meals well seasoned, so I started to add a little spice or some herbs to Maya's food—a pinch of cumin in with the carrots, a few basil leaves in the green beans. She was thrilled with these new additions. And *I* was thrilled that I only needed to spend an hour or two on Sunday preparing Maya's meals for the entire week. I simply popped them into the freezer until it was time to eat—and when Maya was hungry, her meals only took minutes to prepare.

Of course, not every recipe was an immediate success. I might have gone a bit overboard with that fennel and raisin risotto, or when I tried to do something interesting with smoked trout. (I will never forget Maya's reaction—or the look on the pediatrician's face when I told him, "Maya loves everything but smoked trout!") But these first months of experimentation were a wonderful journey for both Maya and me, traveling through tastes and discoveries together.

Up until this point, my story resembles those of many other parents who cook. But mine was about to take another turn. It all started one day when I was visiting a friend with Maya. My friend told me that her son Hugo, eight months at the time, was really picky about food—especially green vegetables, which he pretty much refused to eat. She was curious to understand how Maya ate everything with such gusto. When I told her about my personal recipes, she asked if I would give her one of my dishes out of the freezer to test on her son. I dropped off some of my Green Bean and Sweet Pea Purée with Basil and she called back the same night, telling me that Hugo had eaten absolutely everything—and with a smile! This happened several times with different friends over the subsequent months. People wanted to know my secret. At one point I thought to myself, *Why is there no alternative between jarred baby food (quick and practical but not necessarily tasty) and homemade baby food (tasty but sometimes time-consuming to make)?* I went home that evening and told my husband that I wanted to quit my stable and well-paid job as a strategy consultant and start a baby food business. He told me I was crazy and gave me the thumbs up (which is one of the reasons I love him so much).

Eighteen months, thousands of work hours, hundreds of doubts, and just as many assurances later, Les Menus Bébé were available for sale at grocery stores across the Paris region. The rest is history.

What you hold in your hands is the result of several years' work. Here are my most successful attempts to bring delectable, nutritious, and balanced food to my babies' table—and now to yours. You'll find all the recipes that Maya and Milo (my son, who arrived three years after Maya) loved the most, all the recipes so easy to make that even *I* couldn't find an excuse not to whip them up—all the recipes that were selected for the Les Menus Bébé line. In this book, you'll also find my "Yummy Tips" and organizational tricks for squeezing baby food cooking into your already busy schedule, ideas for how to help your baby love all kinds of tastes and textures, and ways you can help him or her become an adventurous, happy, and healthy eater.

So thank you for picking up this book. Thank you for deciding that what your baby eats is important. Thank you for believing that taste is one of the most important senses we have. Thank you for wanting to share your culinary traditions and nutritional convictions with your little one. Thank you for taking the time to help your baby learn to love all the yummy tastes of nature. Thank you, Super Parent! You're doing a great job.

Love,

Jenny

Introduction

Dr. Jean Lalau Keraly, Pediatric Nutritionist and Endocrinologist

passing on the pleasure of eating

As a pediatrician specializing in childhood nutrition and obesity, after twenty years of practice I've noticed that the concept of pleasure is at least as important in nutrition—and in the treatment of nutrition-related illnesses—as the foods themselves. It's never too early, or too late, to introduce a child to the world of flavors. It's the one thing that will enable him or her, as an adult, to see healthy eating not as an obligation, but as a true pleasure.

make mealtime something special

How many times in my office have I listened to mothers' sighs of regret as they blame themselves for not having taken the time to prepare their baby's first purées! Commercial baby food is successful, even if none of us is foolish enough to believe that it's a cure-all. While it is practical, economical, and hygienic, mass-market baby food has a long way to go in terms of taste, and creativity. Taking the time to prepare your baby's meals helps make mealtime something special.

ambiance and appetite

It's something I notice every day in my line of work: The environment in which a child eats determines her appetite, conditions her interest in her meal, her desire to taste, and even the general way in which she understands food. A child's mealtime is all too often punctuated with bouts of crying, threats, worry, and indifference. It's no wonder many babies are not so inclined to discover new foods.

baby meals for a baby revolution

When I met Jenny Carenco during a pediatric consultation, I was immediately impressed by the epicurean vision that she wanted to pass on to her daughter as well as the daring baby food recipes she was trying out. I tried to share my knowledge of nutrition and pediatrics with her, and to be a source of reassurance and encouragement when she was having doubts. And like any mother who has decided to achieve something on her baby's behalf, she did amazing things! But she wanted more: to give all parents access to the baby recipes she had devised. Her objective: to reconcile—perhaps for the first time—practicality with an explosion of flavors in order to lead a new generation on the path to natural, varied, and balanced foods.

(re)discovering the pleasure of "homemade"

The challenge was clear and I immediately jumped on board, seizing the chance to collaborate with Jenny and contribute to changing things for the better. I regularly see children in my office who have never bitten into an apple—children for whom the food universe consists mainly of sugary foods and pasta. Today, commercial food for children that contains added sugar—baby food included—locks our children into a reassuring-yet-dangerous spiral in which everything is sugary and uniform in taste. Supporting Jenny's gutsy project was taking a step toward the first true alternative since Gerber's "homemade" baby food jars appeared in 1930. It also meant offering hurried parents a real path to feeding their little ones naturally. Finally, it presented an opportunity for the beginning of a change in the general mind-set and an awakening of the parental consciousness.

taking control of your family's diet

This book completes the picture. Jenny was looking for a way to prepare balanced meals for her baby, and this book includes all that she has learned along the way so that parents like you finally have a true resource. This book shows parents how to take control of their family's diet, from the baby to the eldest child, without giving up too much in return. It playfully expounds on the joys of eating, instilling the basics of healthy food consumption, cleverly fitting into modern parents' lifestyles, and encouraging them to take an educational trip along the unknown—and somewhat frightening—path of the "homemade." You hold in your hands a guide to helping your children become healthy eaters—the only reliable weapon against obesity and rampant food disorders. Let's get cooking!

the secret to successful baby cuisine? organization!

A bit clichéd, maybe, yet it's completely true. In order to keep your sanity (and get some sleep), your only life preserver is a well-thought-out plan. You'll see: By integrating the techniques and recipes into your routine bit by bit, you will be able to follow it without even thinking. And it's at this moment that you'll say to yourself, "In fact, making food for my brood is not witchcraft!" But before we get there, let's do a quick theoretical trial run. A champion's logistical foundations can be enumerated on only one hand:

rule 1: always have a supply of "savior foods" on hand

Why saviors? Because if you always have them in stock, they'll be your lifesavers, enabling you to pull together healthy, quick, and delicious recipes for the whole family! Without these culinary basics, each recipe will feel like Mount Everest, forcing you to shop every day for one or two missing ingredients—a real nightmare for a working parent. So be sure to have a few savior foods in your pantry (see pages 16–19).

rule 2: pool recipes

Sure, you are going to cook these recipes for your baby. But look at it from another angle: The vegetables or ingredients that you're going to prepare for your budding gourmet can also serve as the basis for your own meals. That way you won't feel as though you're spending the whole night in the kitchen, dreaming up separate meals for your baby, the older children, and for the evening *tête-à-tête* with your partner. Share the wealth! For almost every recipe in this book, I've given you "Yummy Tips" for transforming the baby recipe into a tasty dish for grown-ups. You can also use the "What Ingredient at What Age?" chart on pages 184–85 (and on the inner front and back covers) for recipe inspiration organized by ingredients and the diner's age.

rule 3: make extra and do less work later

Let's be honest. There are evenings when even the most organized of parents simply doesn't have the twenty minutes it takes to prepare a simple meal: think never-ending managers' meeting, massive traffic jam, incubating flu . . . Don't panic. The perfect planner in you has already prepared for this possibility. Just take one of your "emergency containers" (that you made up on one of your more courageous days) out of the freezer. If you're worried you'll never have one of those courageous days to devote expressly to cooking the emergency supplies, no problem. My extreme laziness also inspired this iron-clad logic: All I had to do was cook larger quantities of baby meals than I needed and freeze the leftovers. See the "Prep/Cook/Storage" box that follows.

rule 4: make a weekly meal plan

Life will be so much easier if you organize your menus for the week ahead. First, you'll be able to do your shopping all at once and avoid the horror of the crowded supermarket on your way home from work. You'll also be able to plan your recipes around your schedule. Are your Tuesday nights cut short by that endless meeting your boss insists on holding at 6 pm? Then put the osso buco on hold and use your always-calm Monday evening to make Tuesday's ratatouille. In one word, *plan* in order to manage your time effectively.

rule 5: make sunday evenings your logistical ally

You'll tell anyone who will listen: I'm sick of Sunday-night films from the eighties! Well, instead of vegetating before the umpteenth showing of *Back to the Future II*, use this night to get a head start on your weekly dinner menus. Putting on your favorite music and spending one hour in the kitchen will save you much needed time during the rest of the week—when you're likely to be feeling tired, stressed, and irritable. Prepare all the sauces that need some time to simmer, then freeze them, leaving only accompaniments like pasta and couscous to cook at the last minute. To be honest, this Sunday cooking time alone with my thoughts and my music is a real escape for me. And when I have to spend only three minutes to reheat those pre-prepared meals, I'm simply ecstatic.

prep/cook/storage

Directly under the title of each recipe, you will notice these four symbols:

🕐   notes a recipe's prep time in minutes

🍲   notes a recipe's cooking time in minutes

▤   notes how long a recipe can be stored in the refrigerator

❄   notes at what temperature (°F) a recipe should be frozen

For example, these symbols indicate that a recipe takes 5 minutes to prep and 10 to cook, can be stored for 24 hours in the refrigerator, and must be frozen at 0°F. You'll notice that all but a handful of special baking recipes at the back of the book take under 30 minutes to prep and cook, and many take under 15 minutes! If you see the ❄ symbol, you'll know that you can plan ahead according to Rule 5 and freeze those meal components in advance.

ESSENTIAL TOOLS

an immersion blender

You'll love this little "giraffe," which will turn your tasty small meals into easy soups for your baby, then into thick purées and finally into chunkier compotes with morsels of whole food. Easy to use and to clean.

a heavy-bottomed pot (with lid)

Invest in this 4-in-1 utensil, which will allow you to reduce a risotto, boil water for pasta, simmer a stew, and brown meat! Perfect for small kitchens.

a vegetable peeler

Better than a knife, since it peels away the flesh in a flash and keeps more of the outer skin, which contains most of the vitamins.

a potato masher

The *only* way to make a potato purée, unless you want to serve potato glue. Find one in your favorite Swedish design-deco store.

a fine strainer

For removing lumps from purées, sauces, and compotes, and for draining pasta and vegetables.

Tupperware containers in various sizes

Easy to use, freeze, reheat, store, and wash, these will simplify your organization, and therefore your life.

aluminum foil

For wrapping up, poaching, baking, or cooking *en papillote* (wrapped and baked in foil or parchment paper). It's an essential item in a cook's drawer.

parchment paper

It's the stuff we're always afraid to put in the oven, but it's made especially for this task—as well as for cooking without burning, for easy removal from the pan to protect food, and for cooking *en papillote*.

freezer bags, with zipper

Indispensable for keeping leftovers in the fridge, storing portions of baby meals, or carrying snacks without having to worry about leaks.

a cutting board and a good knife

Choose a big plastic cutting board that's flexible enough to let you transfer cut-up vegetables into the pot without losing half of them.

ESSENTIAL TOOLS

pantry essentials

These are your "pantry essentials," the items that you use regularly and should always have on hand. Keep stock of them to make sure you never run out. A bimonthly purchase should do it.

raisins

apricots or prunes

honey

ground cumin, ginger, allspice, cinnamon

sugar

baking powder

LE VÉRITABLE
ALCIET ROSE
DEPUIS 1897

LEVURE CHIMIQUE
"ALSACIENNE"
MARQUES DÉPOSÉES
DOSE POUR 500 G DE FARINE

olive oil

pasta

brown sugar

flour

crunchy or plain muesli

couscous and polenta

Basmati and Arborio (round Italian) rice

frozen in advance

These are your "frozen friends," the fresh items you've frozen ahead of time to simplify your life. They will keep for a long time, yet still retain the flavor and nutritional value present in fresh-picked fruits and vegetables.

summer berries and exotic fruits: mangos, lychees, pineapple . . .

aromatic fresh herbs (basil, chives, tarragon, thyme, and cilantro) and chopped shallots and garlic

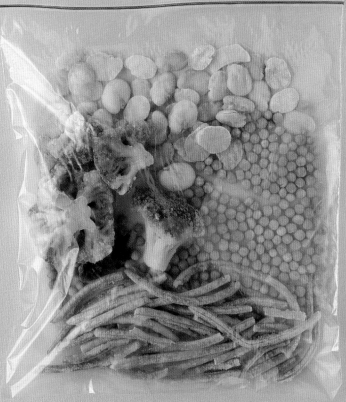

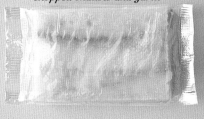

fish fillets (cod, salmon, tuna) and white chicken meat

green vegetables: peas, broccoli, fava beans, green beans, spinach

fresh dairy

This is your "must-have" basket, the list of things you should get in the habit of buying every time you go to the supermarket. They'll become instinctive purchases.

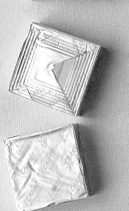

grated Parmesan

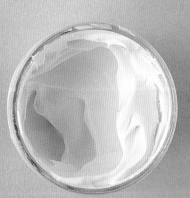

milk

*fromage blanc
or plain,
unsweetened
Greek yogurt*

*crème fraîche (or cream cheese
will do in a pinch)*

*soft cheese, such
as Laughing Cow*

butter

fresh fruits and vegetables

Here's your ticket to healthy pleasure. Keep these treasures on hand in small quantities in your crisper drawer for meals that are rich in taste. Replenish your supply weekly.

oranges and clementines

apples

bananas

tomatoes: regular and cherry

don't forget seasonal berries!

zucchini

potatoes

carrots

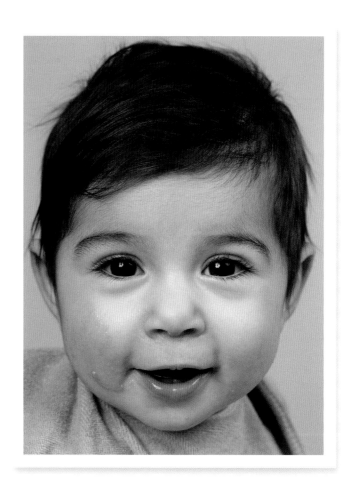

Mona,
6 months, baby foodie

first compotes

&

first purées

starting from 4 months of age
(but fine if you don't start until 6 months)

Discovering Food

Dr. Jean Lalau Keraly, Pediatric Nutritionist and Endocrinologist

when should I introduce solid food?

It's the big question that gnaws at parents—some worrying that their little gourmand will be deprived or undernourished if they don't give him his first purée the day he turns four months old. Others see potential allergens everywhere—even in foods as innocuous as the green bean, so they subject it to appalling culinary transformations intended to rid the bean of its potential toxicity and its vitamins at the same time.

listen to your baby!

You know it's time to give your baby his first fruits or vegetables when he starts to be interested in them! Is he starting to balk at drinking his whole bottle around five months? Does he stretch out his hand to grab at whatever's on your plate or ask for the crust of bread you're about to crunch on? It's without a doubt the time to let him taste his first compotes. Are you stamping your feet with impatience at the idea of having your six-month-old taste that carrot purée, even though he's still greedily sucking his bottle and clamps his mouth shut whenever you approach him with a spoonful of food? Try again later! Between four and six months, there's no hurry: Milk remains his staple food, which will help him grow properly. The first meals are an initiation to flavors and to the pleasure of eating, not yet (or at least not very much) a real nutritional contribution.

the path to a varied diet

Fruits or vegetables first? It's the question parents always ask pediatricians. In order to give parents a better response than "it makes no difference," pediatricians have divided themselves into two camps, "veggies first" and "fruit first," and each side has excellent arguments. In reality, as long as you introduce your little one to a food, it doesn't matter if it's a vegetable or a fruit. Simply avoid at-risk foods—meaning those with strong potential for allergies, foods such as egg whites, strawberries, and nuts.

let your baby follow his own rhythm

Certain parents worry when they see their baby refusing to eat the suggested cereals and grains prescribed by official nutritional guidelines. What's the difference, if their little one is in good health? During the discovery phase, offer your baby what awakens his curiosity and makes him happy. Let him get to know foods, and don't worry if he doesn't always finish the portion size prescribed by your pediatrician: Milk will fill in any nutritional gaps.

is he asking for more carrots?

Give him some more. Your role is to introduce him to fruits and vegetables, which is pure pleasure! Offer him fruits or veggies depending on what you're in the mood to cook as well as whatever your baby is asking for. Is it hot outside? Opt for a peach compote. It's cold? Whip up a yummy broccoli purée. Start with gentle variations, at first proposing a single new food every three or four days, in order to monitor your baby's reactions. If all goes well, keep going by introducing other foods.

never force your child

If you do, you run the risk of compromising his future relationship to food. Instead, simply put out prepared fruits and vegetables, and observe his reaction to them. Finally, don't hesitate to invite your baby to join you at the dinner table so he can familiarize himself with your (positive) eating habits and enter into the "grown-up" dynamic. And if, on top of it all, he discovers that you're eating the same thing he is, it's a pretty good bet that Baby will quickly, successfully, and excitedly enter the magical world of food.

a special note to changephobes

To parents worried about the potential danger of certain foods, I'll say this: You cannot put your child in a protective bubble and forcibly keep him in an infantile state. The passage to solid food is a turning point in his development of motor skills. Food in itself is not dangerous, even if Baby winds up having a food allergy. Simply take your time so that Baby can get used to a range of fruits and vegetables. This way, you can control his reactions and adjust his diet according to his needs. Finally, realize that holding back the introduction of solid food (beyond seven to eight months) means taking the risk of exposing your child to nutritional deficiencies or eating behavior problems.

and a special note to the change determined

To those who want to introduce solid food too early (before four months of age), be aware that this means replacing a whole food—milk—with something of inferior quality, which is likely to cause problems of variable degrees. It's only after four months of age that a baby's digestive system is mature enough to process anything besides milk. By then his intestinal mucus membrane is reinforced, reducing the risks of food allergy. The suction reflex has diminished and his muscular coordination has improved, allowing Baby to use his tongue to push the purées into his throat before swallowing them.

peach compote
compote de pêches

⏱	🍲	🗄	❄
5	10	24ʰ	0°

Makes five 3½-ounce (100 g) servings

*12 yellow peaches,
about 1⅓ pounds (600 g)*

1. Wash the peaches, remove the pits, and slice the fruit.
2. Put the peaches into a saucepan, cover the fruit one third of the way with water, and bring to a boil. Cover and cook over medium heat for 10 minutes. When done, 3 to 4 tablespoons of liquid should remain.
3. Blend to obtain a smooth compote.

yummy tips

You can add 1 or 2 fresh mint leaves to the compote when it's finished cooking.

Peaches render a lot of water. If there's too much liquid left in the saucepan, set it aside. It makes a sweet all-natural syrup you can use instead of sugar as a dessert topping for yogurt or cottage cheese.

apple compote
compote de pommes

| 10 | 15 | 24ʰ | 0° |

Makes five 3½-ounce (100 g) servings

5 to 6 sweet apples (McIntosh, Golden Delicious, Fuji), about 1⅓ pounds (600 g)

1. Wash and peel the apples, remove the cores and any spare seeds, then cut the fruit into cubes.
2. Put the apples into a saucepan, cover the fruit halfway with water, and bring to a boil. Cook, uncovered, over medium heat for 15 minutes. When done, 3 or 4 tablespoons of liquid should remain.
3. Make sure the apples are well cooked before blending them to obtain a smooth compote.

yummy tips

To change things up, you can add ½ teaspoon of cinnamon to the apples while they're cooking. My children also love when I add bananas to the apples in this recipe. To do this, replace 2 apples with 2 peeled bananas. Cut the bananas into small slices. Follow the same cooking guidelines and blend. Delicious!

pear compote
compote de poires

| 7 | 15 | 24ʰ | 0° |

Makes five 3½-ounce (100 g) servings

6 big pears (Bosc, Bartlett, Williams), about 1⅓ pounds (600 g)

1. Wash and peel the pears, remove the cores and any spare seeds, then cut the fruit into cubes.
2. Put the pears into a saucepan, cover the fruit halfway with water, and bring to a boil. Cook, uncovered, over medium heat for 15 minutes. When done, 3 or 4 tablespoons of liquid should remain.
3. Make sure the pears are well cooked before blending them to obtain a smooth compote.

yummy tips

This purée tastes even better if you add a vanilla bean while the pears are cooking. With a knife, open 1 vanilla bean lengthwise and scrape it to remove the seeds. Throw the seeds into the saucepan along with the open bean. Before blending, remove the bean. For a caramelized flavor for babies twelve months and up, add 4 tablespoons of honey 2 or 3 minutes before removing the pears from the heat. Stir the honey well once added so it doesn't stick to the saucepan. Blend as described above.

apricot compote

compote d'abricots

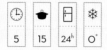

5	15	24ʰ	0°

Makes five 3½-ounce (100 g) servings

15 apricots, about 1⅓ pounds (600 g)

1. Wash and peel the apricots, remove the seeds, then cut the flesh into pieces.
2. Put the apricots into a saucepan, cover the fruit halfway with water, and bring to a boil. Cover and cook the apricots over medium heat for 15 minutes. When done, 3 or 4 tablespoons of liquid should remain.
3. Blend until you have a smooth compote.

yummy tips

Apricots go very well with vanilla. With a knife, open 1 vanilla bean lengthwise and scrape it to remove the seeds. Throw the seeds into the saucepan along with the open bean. Before blending, remove the bean.

Another option: Add 2 basil leaves before blending. Try this variation for yourself as an accompaniment to grilled meat or served with goat cheese.

melon compote
compote de melon

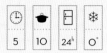

| 5 | 10 | 24ʰ | 0° |

Makes five 3½-ounce (100 g) servings

1 melon (cantaloupe or other varieties), about 1⅓ pounds (600 g)

1. Cut the melon in half, remove the seeds, then slice the halves into crescent moons. Cut away the rind, then slice the fruit into rectangular pieces.
2. Blend for a refreshing no-cook compote.

For a more intense flavor, roast the melon in the oven first. Doing so reduces the amount of water in the fruit and enhances its flavor.
1. Preheat the oven to 400°F (200°C).
2. Follow step 1 in the directions above.
3. Put the melon pieces, without the rind, in a baking dish and cover with aluminum foil.
4. Roast in the oven for 20 minutes.
5. Remove the melon from the oven, let cool, and blend until you have a smooth compote.

yummy tips

Try the roasted version using watermelon. Follow the recipe above, but double the quantity of fruit and make sure you remove all of the black seeds. For adults, this compote is an excellent dessert with a scoop of vanilla ice cream and chopped basil leaves.

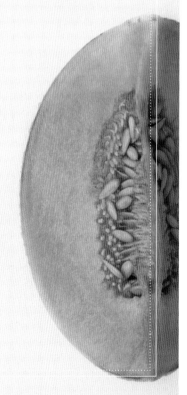

yellow (mirabelle) plum compote
compote de mirabelles

⏰	🍲	🗄	❄
5	15	24ʰ	0°

Makes five 3½-ounce (100 g) servings

6 to 8 yellow (Mirabelle) plums, about 1⅔ pounds (750 g)

1. Wash the plums and cut them into halves. Remove the pits.
2. Put the plums into a saucepan, cover the fruit halfway with water, and bring to a boil. Cover and cook over low heat for 10 to 15 minutes.
3. When done, 3 or 4 tablespoons of liquid should remain. If there's more, you can use it as a natural sweetener to top off dairy desserts. If there's not enough, add a few spoonfuls of water.
4. Blend into a smooth compote.

yummy tips

For babies over twelve months, add 2 tablespoons of honey halfway through the cooking time for a sweet snack. For slightly older children, you can sprinkle brown sugar in place of honey on the unsweetened compote just before serving for a little crunchiness. If yellow plums are out of season, use frozen plums, which are excellent for making compotes.

mango-banana compote
compote mangues-bananes

5   10   24ʰ   0°

Makes five 3½-ounce (100 g) servings

2 ripe mangoes, about 14 ounces (400 g) mango flesh
3 bananas

1. Cut off the sides of the mangoes along either side of the pit. With a small knife, remove the skin from both sides and cut the flesh into pieces. Trim the flesh from around the pit and remove the skin.
2. Remove the banana peels and slice the fruit into small rounds.
3. Put the mango pieces and bananas into a saucepan, cover the fruit halfway with water, and bring to a boil. Cover and cook over low heat for 10 minutes. When done, about 3 tablespoons of liquid will remain.
4. Blend until you have a smooth compote.

yummy tips

Frozen mango (available skinned and sliced) is often less expensive and more practical to use than fresh. Perfect for a compote!

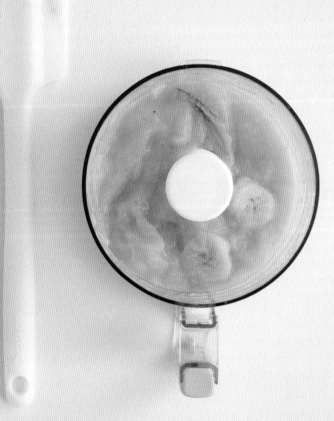

pineapple and lychee compote
compote ananas-litchis

15 20 24ʰ 0°

Makes five 3½ ounce (100 g) servings

1 pineapple, about ⅔ pound (300 g) pineapple flesh
16 lychees (200 g), fresh or frozen

1. Peel the pineapple until every bit of skin has been removed from the fruit. Cut around the hard core to remove it, then cut the flesh of the pineapple into cubes.
2. Peel the lychees, if using fresh ones, and remove the pits.
3. Put the pineapple and lychees into a saucepan, cover the fruit halfway with water, and bring to a boil. Cover and cook over low heat for 20 minutes. When done cooking, about 3 tablespoons of liquid should remain.
4. Blend until you have a smooth compote.

yummy tips

Since this was my daughter's favorite compote when she was little, I made it often. You can easily find ready-to-use frozen pineapple and lychees all year round—both are much more practical than fresh fruit.

cherry and apple compote

compote cerises-pommes

| 20 | 15 | 24ʰ | 0° |

Makes five 3½ ounce (100 g) servings

*About 14 ounces (400 g) cherries
3 large apples (Belle de Boskoop or
Golden Delicious),
about ⅔ pound (300 g)*

1. Wash the cherries, then remove the stems and pits with a small knife.
2. Wash and peel the apples, remove the cores and any spare seeds, and cut the fruit in cubes.
3. Put the cherries and apples into a saucepan, cover the fruit halfway with water, and bring to a boil. Cover and cook over medium heat for 15 minutes. When done, about 3 tablespoons of liquid should remain.
4. Blend until you have a smooth compote.

yummy tips

Out of season, you can replace the cherries with red grapes. Wash and cut them in half, and remove any seeds. Use sweet apples (such as Golden Delicious) to balance the slight acidity of the grapes.

plum and pear compote

compote prunes-poires

15   15   24ʰ   0°

Makes five 3½-ounce (100 g) servings

3 to 4 plums, about ¾ pound (350 g)
3 sweet pears (such as Williams), about
⅔ pound (300 g)

1. Wash the plums and remove the pits with a small knife.
2. Wash and peel the pears, remove the cores and any spare seeds, and cut the flesh into cubes.
3. Put the plums and pears in a saucepan, cover the fruit one-third of the way with water, and bring to a boil. Cover and cook over medium heat for 15 minutes. When done, about 3 tablespoons of liquid should remain.
4. Blend until you have a smooth compote.

yummy tips

Many different kinds of plums exist, some more acidic than others. Use well-ripened plums. They are sweeter, and their skin will add a slightly sour note.

carrot purée
purée de carottes

10	15	24ʰ	O°

Makes five 3½-ounce (100 g) servings

8 carrots, just over 1 pound (500 g)
1 teaspoon sunflower oil

1. Wash and peel the carrots, then chop them into small rounds.
2. Put the carrots into a saucepan, cover them with water, and bring to a boil. Cover and cook over medium heat for 15 minutes.
3. Drain the carrots and blend them with the sunflower oil until smooth.

yummy tips

Carrots sometimes lose a little of their sweetness when cooked. To enhance their natural flavor, add a few fresh cilantro leaves just before blending. For an Middle Eastern touch, cook the carrots in ¾ cup and 2 tablespoons (200 ml) orange juice. After cooking, blend the carrots with the remaining orange juice, ½ teaspoon of ground cumin, and for bébé gourmets over twelve months, a few drops of honey. Even grown-ups love it!

broccoli purée
purée de brocolis

5   10   24ʰ   0°

Makes five 3½-ounce (100 g) servings

8 cups (600 g) broccoli florets,
fresh or frozen
1 teaspoon olive oil

1. Wash the florets, if you are using fresh broccoli.
2. Put the broccoli into a saucepan. Cover the broccoli halfway with water, bring to a boil, and cook, uncovered, over medium heat for 10 minutes. When done, about 2 tablespoons of water should remain.
3. Blend the broccoli with the remaining cooking water and the olive oil until smooth.

yummy tips

To make this strong-tasting purée sweeter and creamier for Bébé, add 2 squares of soft cheese (such as Laughing Cow) just before blending. You can also add a few leaves of fresh flat-leaf parsley or sage before blending.

sweet pea purée
purée de petits pois

5   10   24ʰ   0°

Makes five 3½-ounce (100 g) servings

3 cups (500 g) peas, fresh or frozen
2 tablespoons crème fraîche

1. Put the peas into a saucepan, cover with water, bring to a boil, and cook over low heat for 7 to 8 minutes. Drain.
2. Blend with the crème fraîche until you have a smooth purée.

yummy tips

For a mildly tangy note, blend this recipe with 2 fresh mint leaves. This version is excellent for Bébé, as well as the rest of the family, with grilled lamb. Some babies don't like the grainy texture that comes from the peas' somewhat thick skin. Personally, I believe that children should get used to the natural textures of food, but if you need to, you can pass the purée through a fine strainer to acquire a smoother mixture.

green bean purée
purée de haricots verts

5 10 24ʰ 0°

Makes five 3½-ounce (100 g) servings

3⅓ cups (500 g) French green beans, fresh or frozen
1 teaspoon olive oil

1. Trim the ends of the green beans, if you are using fresh ones.
2. Put the green beans into a saucepan, cover them halfway with water, bring to a boil, cover, and cook over medium heat for 10 minutes. When done, about 2 tablespoons of water should remain.
3. Blend the green beans with the remaining cooking water and the olive oil until smooth.

yummy tips

You can also make this purée by replacing half the green beans with sweet peas. The result will be slightly creamier and sweeter than the original recipe. For a taste of summer, add 2 fresh basil leaves before blending either version of this recipe.

avocado purée
purée d'avocat

5   5

Makes one 3½-ounce
(100 g) serving

1 ripe avocado
2 to 3 drops lemon juice

1. Cut open the avocado and remove the pit.
2. Scoop out the avocado flesh with a spoon and put it into a bowl.
3. Mash the flesh with the lemon juice (to preserve the green color) until you have a smooth purée.

yummy tips

Unlike other fruits, avocados ripen once picked, not on the tree. A hard avocado is therefore a sign of freshness! To ripen them, simply leave at room temperature in a brown paper bag. To speed the process, place a banana or apple in the bag along with the avocado.

My daughter Maya still devours this purée with chicken, grilled meat, or fish such as tuna or swordfish. Now that she's older, we add a pinch of sea salt and a drop of Tabasco to her "kiddie guacamole."

sweet potato purée
purée de patates douces

5	15	24ʰ	0°

Makes five 3½-ounce (100 g) servings

2½ sweet potatoes, about 1⅓ pounds (600 g)
1 scant tablespoon (10 g) butter

1. Wash and peel the sweet potatoes, then cut them into cubes.
2. Put the cubes into a saucepan, cover them with water, bring to a boil, and cook over medium heat for 15 minutes. Drain.
3. Blend with the butter until you have a smooth purée.

yummy tips

Sweet potatoes are a favorite with kids. For older babies I often cut the sweet potatoes into *batons* (fries) and roast them in the oven for about 20 minutes. The flavor becomes even more pronounced, and kids love to eat with their fingers!

parsnip purée
purée de panais

Makes five 3½-ounce (100 g) servings

9 parsnips, about 1⅓ pounds (600 g)
¾ cup and 2 tablespoons (200 ml) milk
1 scant tablespoon (10 g) butter

1. Wash and peel the parsnips, then cut them into cubes.
2. Put the cubes into a saucepan, cover with milk, bring the milk to a boil, stirring constantly, then lower heat, cover, and cook over medium heat for 15 minutes. Drain, keeping a bit of the drained milk aside.
3. Blend with the butter and a little of the cooking milk until you have a smooth, creamy purée.

yummy tips

You can vary this recipe by replacing 1 parsnip with a sweet apple (Fuji or similar). Add the peeled, cored, and cubed apples 5 minutes before the end of the cooking time. Drain the excess milk so that the purée is not too wet, then blend. This purée is sweeter and fruitier than most, so it's great for even the smallest babies. I serve it with beef bourguignon or lamb cutlets to older children.

cauliflower purée

purée de chou-fleur

⏰	🍲	🗄	❄
5	15	24ʰ	0°

Makes five 3½-ounce (100 g) servings

8 cups (600 g) cauliflower florets, fresh or frozen
¾ cup and 2 tablespoons (200 ml) milk
1 scant tablespoon (10 g) butter

1. Wash the cauliflower florets, if you are using fresh.
2. In a saucepan, bring the milk to a boil, add the cauliflower, and cook over medium heat for 15 minutes (be careful, as the milk can boil over easily).
3. Drain off the milk and set aside.
4. Blend the cauliflower with the butter, adding a little of the cooking milk until you have a smooth, creamy purée.

yummy tips

Add a sprig of fresh thyme 5 minutes before the end of the cooking time, and remove the sprig before blending. The thyme will add sweetness without overpowering the taste of the cauliflower.

pumpkin purée
purée de potiron

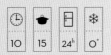

10   15   24ʰ   0°

Makes five 3½-ounce (100 g) servings

1⅔ pounds (750 g) pumpkin
1 large fingerling potato
1 scant tablespoon (10 g) butter
2 to 3 drops lemon juice

1. Wash and peel the pumpkin and potato. Deseed the pumpkin and cut the vegetables into small cubes. It will seem like a lot of pumpkin, but pumpkin loses a lot of water when it cooks.
2. Put the cubes into a saucepan, cover them with water, bring to a boil, and cook over medium heat for 15 minutes. Drain.
3. Blend the vegetable mixture with the butter and lemon juice until you have a smooth purée.

yummy tips

The taste of pumpkin can sometimes be a bit earthy. The lemon juice adds the touch of acidity needed for balance while bringing out the pumpkin's natural taste.

This purée is even better with a pinch of ground cumin or some fresh vanilla. If you opt for cumin, add ¼ teaspoon ground cumin before blending. For the vanilla, slice open a bean, scrape out the seeds with a knife, and add the seeds to the pumpkin and potato just before blending.

potato and corn purée

purée de maïs et pommes de terre

8	10	24ʰ	0°

Makes five 3½-ounce (100 g) servings

2 potatoes, about 1 pound (450 g)
2⅓ cups (400 g) corn, frozen or canned
1 scant tablespoon (10 g) butter

1. Wash and peel the potatoes, then cut them into cubes.
2. Put the cubes into a saucepan, cover them with water, and bring to a boil.
3. Add the corn and cook the vegetables over medium heat for 10 minutes. Drain.
4. Blend the vegetable mixture with the butter until you have a smooth purée.

yummy tips

For a change, use carrots instead of potatoes. As with green peas, the corn skin creates a slightly grainy purée. If Bébé doesn't like it, pass the purée through a fine strainer before serving.

Milo, 7 months, tester

first lunches
&
first sweets

6 months+

First Lunches

Dr. Jean Lalau Keraly, Pediatric Nutritionist and Endocrinologist

In just a few months, your baby has adjusted to a new diet: Now she eats real portions of vegetables at lunch and some fruit as an afternoon snack, even though milk is still her main food source. She's becoming more independent, serving herself—more or less skillfully—with her own spoon. In the evening she delights in her bottle of milk sometimes accompanied by a bit of cereal, depending on her appetite.

introduction of new foods

By the age of six or seven months, your baby can take another step on the path to eating like a grown-up: You can introduce meat, fish, cereals, cheese, and other dairy besides milk into her diet. The arrival of these new foods means parents can offer more interesting recipes and elaborate choices. It also means they can begin to mesh Baby's meals with the family's, delighting the baby because such a move indicates that her social status in the family has risen. It's fun for the parents, as well, since it makes for simpler meal logistics.

ever so slowly

If you have introduced meat into the diet of your six- or seven-month-old baby, make sure you don't turn her into a first-class carnivore! At this age, 2 teaspoons (20 g) a day of animal protein will do for her body. You can serve up to 3 teaspoons at this time, if your baby seems to be a big fan. This is the time to serve your mini-gourmet more elaborate lunches with mixed meat or fish, along with a side dish, so Baby can differentiate the textures, colors, and flavors of the food. The meal naturally ends with a sweet touch—a small serving of fruit compote or crushed fruit—and why not mix in some fromage blanc or plain, unsweetened Greek yogurt?

respect your baby's appetite, desires, and preferences

If she doesn't finish eating, don't force her. If she wants more vegetables, give her some. Unlike we adults, who are capable of serving ourselves three helpings of Aunt Monica's lasagna—with extra sauce, please, Auntie!—your baby knows how to listen to her body when she's eaten enough. If she's no longer hungry, she'll refuse dessert (even if that seems inconceivable to you). If she doesn't like the corn compote that you lovingly prepared, don't take it personally.

You can have her try it again some other time. She has the right, just as you do, not to like certain foods, and her tastes will evolve. The simple rule is just to have her taste.

at 7 months

Your baby can start eating eggs. Only serve the egg yolk, however, since the white can be allergenic and is not recommended before a baby is at least a year old (three years old if the child has a history of allergies). Start by offering half of the yolk (well cooked).

at 8 months

You can let your baby chew on a crust of bread, which will help with teething. Always sit next to your little one as she nibbles her bread. If she bites off a piece that's too big, she won't be able to spit it out herself. If you're worried about an accident, try rice cakes instead. They are just as pleasurable for the baby but are safer since the rice grains break off as the child chews.

in this chapter

You are going to discover real lunches that mark a new era of tasty discoveries for your baby. This is the time of flavor association and more complex recipes that are bolder than before. As your baby's taste buds awaken, you will teach her how to accept and appreciate new things, a talent she will carry late into life. She will not become the kind of person who relies solely on starchy staple foods like rice and pasta.

chicken with carrots and apricots

poulet aux carottes et abricots

15   20   24ʰ   0°

Makes five 3½-ounce (100 g) servings

10 carrots, about 1⅓ pounds (600 g)
10 to 12 apricots, fresh or frozen,
about ⅔ pound (300 g)
1 chicken breast, about 3½ ounces (100 g)
1 teaspoon sunflower oil
2 teaspoons finely chopped shallots
¾ cup and 2 tablespoons (200 ml)
orange juice

1. Wash and peel the carrots, then cut them into rounds.
2. Wash and pit the apricots.
3. Cut the chicken breast into small pieces.
4. In a heavy-bottomed saucepan, heat the oil over medium heat and add the shallots. Brown them for 1 to 2 minutes, then add the chicken breast pieces.
5. Once the chicken pieces are browned on all sides, add the carrots, the apricots, and the orange juice. Add water to cover the mixture halfway.
6. Bring to a boil, reduce the heat, cover, and let simmer for 15 to 20 minutes. Check to make sure the carrots are tender before removing from the heat.
7. Blend to a smooth purée.

accompaniments

Serve this dish with Parsnip Purée (page 43), Turnip Purée (page 68), or Sweet Pea Purée (page 39).

yummy tips

You can replace the fresh or frozen fruit with 10 dried apricots, but you will need to double the amount of orange juice used. Not only are dried apricots easily found in stores year-round, they also have the advantage of being very rich in iron and in vitamin B.

chicken and tarragon fricassee

fricassée de poulet à l'estragon

Makes five 3½-ounce (100 g) servings

½ turnip, just under ¼ pound (100 g)
2 zucchini, about ¼ pound (120 g)
1½ cups (100 g) broccoli florets
½ cup (80 g) green beans
1 chicken breast, about 3½ ounces (100 g)
1 teaspoon sunflower oil
¼ cup (60 ml) vegetable stock
2 teaspoons chopped fresh tarragon

1. Wash the vegetables and peel the turnips and zucchini.
2. Cut the turnips into cubes and the zucchini into rounds.
3. Cut the chicken breast into pieces.
4. In a heavy-bottomed saucepan, heat the oil over medium heat and brown the pieces of chicken. Add the vegetables, stock, and tarragon, then cover the ingredients halfway with water and bring to a boil. Cook over medium heat for 10 minutes.
5. Remove from the heat and drain, reserving some of the cooking liquid. Blend until you have a smooth purée. Add a little of the cooking liquid if the mixture is too dense or grainy.

accompaniments

Serve this dish with Sweet Potato Purée (page 42) or Carrot and Cumin Purée (page 67).

yummy tips

Want to show off for the whole family? Turn this recipe into Chicken Stuffed with Tarragon and Prosciutto. Count on 5 ounces (150 g) of chicken breast per person. Cut an opening in each breast at its thickest point, making a pocket without cutting the chicken completely in two. Cook the vegetables with the tarragon according to the recipe above, drain, and blend to make a dense purée. Place each chicken breast on a slice of prosciutto, then spoon some vegetable purée into the opening. Roll the breast to close the pocket and wrap the ham around the chicken, securing it with a couple of toothpicks. Preheat the oven to 400°F (200°C) and bake for 10 to 12 minutes. Remove the toothpicks and cut the chicken in two to reveal the pretty stuffing. Serve with a mixed green salad and bread spread with fresh goat cheese.

turkey with corn and sweet onions

dinde au maïs et aux oignons doux

⏰	🍲	🗄	❄
5	20	24ʰ	0°

Makes five 3½-ounce (100 g) servings

1 turkey cutlet, about 3½ ounces (100 g)
2 teaspoons sunflower oil
2 tablespoons finely chopped sweet white onions
2 cups (350 g) corn, frozen or canned

1. Cut the turkey cutlet into small pieces.
2. In a heavy-bottomed saucepan, heat the oil over medium heat, add the sweet onions, and cook for 1 minute. Add the turkey pieces and brown them on all sides while stirring nonstop. Add the corn, mix well, and cover the mixture halfway with water.
3. Bring to a boil, reduce the heat, cover, and let simmer over low heat for 15 minutes.
4. Remove from the heat and blend until you have a smooth purée.
5. If the texture is too grainy, add a few spoonfuls of water and blend to your desired consistency.

accompaniments

Serve this dish with Mashed Pumpkin and Apple (page 66) or Sweet Potato Purée (page 42).

yummy tips

Transform this recipe into a risotto for the whole family: Brown ½ cup (100 g) of Arborio rice with the sweet onions and sunflower oil. Add just over ½ cup (120 ml) of water, a ½ cup of chicken stock, and the corn. Stir regularly until the water is absorbed and the rice is tender. In a frying pan, brown the turkey pieces (about 2½ ounces/70 g per person) in 2 teaspoons of sunflower oil and 2 teaspoons lemon juice. When the rice is cooked, add just under ¼ cup (50 g) grated Parmesan, 1 scant tablespoon (10 g) butter, and 5 chopped fresh sage leaves. Before serving, mix the turkey into the risotto.

turkey with chestnuts and apples
dinde aux marrons et pommes

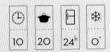

Makes five 3½-ounce (100 g) servings

4 apples, about 14 ounces (400 g)
1 turkey cutlet, about 3½ ounces (100 g)
2 teaspoons finely chopped shallots
1 teaspoon sunflower oil
½ teaspoon cinnamon
½ teaspoon freshly grated ginger
½ teaspoon cloves
1 cup (200 g) precooked chestnuts

1. Wash and peel the apples, remove the cores and any spare seeds, and cut the fruit into pieces.
2. Cut the turkey cutlet into pieces, then brown them in a saucepan over medium heat with the shallots and sunflower oil.
3. Add the spices, stirring with the turkey pieces for about one minute to distribute, then add the apples and chestnuts. Fill the pan halfway with water, bring to a boil, and lower the heat. Cover and simmer for 15 minutes.
4. Remove from the heat and blend until you have a smooth purée.

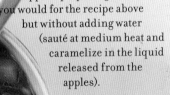

accompaniments
Serve this dish with Sweet Potato Purée (page 42) or Carrot and Cumin Purée (page 67).

yummy tips
Want to prepare this recipe for family members who are one year and up? Child's play! Count on 5 ounces (150 g) of turkey cutlet per person. Preheat the oven to 400°F (200°C). Place the cutlets in an ovenproof dish, combine a few drops of honey, orange juice, and low-sodium soy sauce and brush the cutlets with the mixture. Bake for 12 to 15 minutes. Serve with a side of sautéed chestnuts and apples, preparing them as you would for the recipe above but without adding water (sauté at medium heat and caramelize in the liquid released from the apples).

orange veal piccata
piccata de veau à l'orange

🕐	🍲	🧊	❄
10	15	24ʰ	0°

Makes five 3½-ounce
(100 g) servings

2 large carrots, about ⅓ pound (180 g)
1 fennel bulb, about ½ pound (250 g)
1 veal cutlet, about 3½ ounces (100 g)
1 teaspoon sunflower oil
1 teaspoon finely chopped shallots
1¼ cups (300 ml) orange juice

1. Wash and peel the carrots, then cut them into rounds. Wash the fennel, then remove the stems and cut the bulb into thin strips. Cut the cutlet into cubes.
2. In a heavy-bottomed saucepan, heat the oil over medium heat, add the shallots and the cubes of veal cutlet, and brown them on all sides.
3. Add the carrots, fennel, and orange juice. Cook, uncovered, over medium heat for 12 minutes, making sure there is enough orange juice in the pan. If not, add a few tablespoons of juice or water to get the right quantity. Turn down the heat or cover the pan if you notice the liquid is evaporating too quickly.
4. Remove from the heat and blend until you have a smooth purée.

accompaniments
Serve this dish with Parsnip Purée (page 43) or Sweet Pea Purée (page 39).

yummy tips
For bigger kids, I serve a veal cutlet, seared for 3 minutes on each side and seasoned with a micropinch of sea salt and several drops of lemon juice. This is accompanied by the carrot, fennel, and orange purée. For the purée, cook the carrots and fennel in orange juice as directed above, then blend.

veal stew with "forgotten" vegetables
mijoté de veau aux légumes oubliés

15	20	24ʰ	0°

Makes five 3½-ounce (100 g) servings

1 rutabaga, just under ½ pound (200 g)
1½ parsnips, just under ¼ pound (100 g)
1 piece celery root, about 2 ounces (60 g)
½ fennel bulb, about 2 ounces (60 g)
1 veal cutlet, about 3½ ounces (100 g)
1 teaspoon sunflower oil
2 teaspoons finely chopped shallots

1. Wash and peel the rutabaga, the parsnips, and the celery root. Wash the fennel and remove the stems.
2. Cut the vegetables into pieces and cut the veal cutlet into cubes.
3. In a saucepan, heat the oil over medium heat, add the shallots and the cubes of veal cutlet, and brown the cubes on all sides. Add the vegetables, cover them halfway with water, and bring to a boil. Reduce the heat, cover the pan, and simmer for 20 minutes. There should be about 3 tablespoons of liquid left in the pan after cooking.
4. Remove from the heat and blend until you have a smooth purée.

accompaniments
Serve this dish with Green Bean Purée (page 40), Broccoli Purée (page 38), or Sweet Pea Purée (page 39).

yummy tips
For bigger kids, brown the veal pieces with the chopped shallots and set aside. Cook the vegetables according to the recipe and blend only the vegetables to make a purée. Serve with whole green beans, broccoli, or sweet peas.

lamb stew with green vegetables

petit navarin d'agneau aux légumes verts

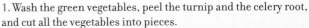

🕐	🍲	🧊	❄
10	25	24ʰ	0°

Makes five 3½-ounce (100 g) servings

1 zucchini, about 2 ounces (60 g)

½ cup (75 g) green beans

¾ cup (50 g) broccoli florets

About ½ cup (75 g) peas, fresh or frozen

½ turnip, just under ¼ pound (100 g)

1 piece celery root, about 1 ounce (30 g)

1 teaspoon sunflower oil

3½ ounces (100 g) lamb shoulder or leg, cut into small pieces

1. Wash the green vegetables, peel the turnip and the celery root, and cut all the vegetables into pieces.
2. In a heavy-bottomed saucepan, heat the oil over medium heat and brown the lamb. Add the turnip and celery root, cover the mixture halfway with water, and bring to a boil. Reduce the heat, cover, and simmer for 15 minutes.
3. Add the green vegetables and cook for another 10 minutes. About 3 tablespoons of liquid should be left in the pan at the end of cooking. If not, pour some out or add a little water to get the right quantity.
4. Remove from the heat and blend until you have a smooth purée.

accompaniments
Serve this dish with Cauliflower Purée (page 44) or Carrot and Cumin Purée (page 67).

yummy tips
For a family of four, use 3½ ounces (100 g) of lamb per person and double the remaining quantities in the recipe. When you add the turnip and celery root, also add 1 cup (240 ml) chicken stock, 1 crushed garlic clove, and 1 teaspoon chopped fresh thyme. Before serving, season with sea salt and freshly ground pepper to taste.

italian beef ragout
ragoût de boeuf à l'italienne

Makes five 3½-ounce (100 g) servings

2 tomatoes, just under ½ pound (200 g)
2 zucchini, about ¼ pound (120 g)
1 celery stalk, about 1 ounce (30 g)
1 carrot, about 2 ounces (60 g)
3½ ounces (100 g) stewing beef
(neck or shoulder)
1 teaspoon olive oil
½ garlic clove, chopped
2 teaspoons tomato paste
½ teaspoon chopped fresh thyme
About ½ cup (120 ml) water

1. Wash the vegetables and peel the carrot. Dice the vegetables and cut the meat into small pieces.
2. In a heavy-bottomed saucepan, heat the olive oil over medium heat and brown the garlic and the beef. Add the vegetables, tomato paste, thyme, and water. Cover and simmer for 25 minutes.
3. Remove from the heat and blend until the ragout has a smooth texture.

accompaniments
Serve with Parsnip Purée (page 43) or Avocado Purée (page 41).

yummy tips
This dish is equally delicious served over pasta. If you decide to try it this way, consider serving it with additional green vegetables, such as green beans.

mini-flan with sweet potato and cod

petit flan de patate douce et cabillaud

⏰	🍲	🗄	❄
10	20	24ʰ	0°

Makes five 3½-ounce (100 g) servings

1 large sweet potato,
about ⅔ pound (300 g)
1 large potato,
just under ¼ pound (100 g)
1 cod fillet, about 5 ounces (150 g)
1 scant tablespoon (10 g) butter
2 fresh sage leaves, finely chopped

1. Wash and peel the potatoes, then cut them into cubes. Put the cubes into a saucepan, cover them with water, and bring to a boil. Reduce the heat, cover, and cook for 15 minutes.
2. Make sure there are no bones in the fish.
3. In a separate saucepan, let the fish fillet simmer in boiling water for 5 minutes.
4. Remove the potatoes from the heat and drain; add the butter and mash until you have a smooth purée.
5. Finely chop the cod and blend with the purée and the sage. Using a ramekin or cooking ring, make the shape of a flan in the middle of Bébé's plate.

accompaniments

Serve this dish with Sweet Pea Purée (page 42), Broccoli Purée (page 38), or Green Bean Purée (page 40).

yummy tips

The rest of the family can enjoy this dish on a cold winter's night as well. Count on 5 ounces (150 g) of cod fillet per person. Put the fillets into an ovenproof dish, add a few teaspoons of olive oil, a few drops of lemon juice, and a pinch of sea salt. Cover with the sweet potato and potato purée. Preheat the oven to 400°F (200°C) and bake for 15 minutes.

salmon with spinach
saumon aux épinards

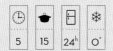

5   15   24ʰ   0°

Makes five 3½-ounce (100 g) servings

1 salmon fillet, about 3½ ounces (100 g)
1 teaspoon lemon juice
3⅓ cups (500 g) frozen spinach
¼ cup vegetable stock (60 ml)
2 tablespoons crème fraîche

1. Make sure there are no bones in the salmon fillet and cut it into small cubes.
2. Put the salmon cubes on a plate and sprinkle them with the lemon juice. Set aside.
3. Put the spinach into a saucepan with the vegetable stock and add water until the spinach is just covered. Bring to a boil. Cover and cook over medium heat for 10 minutes. Add the salmon cubes and cook for 5 minutes more.
4. Drain the mixture and put back on the heat in the saucepan. Add the crème fraîche, mix well, and allow to heat through.
5. Blend until you have a smooth purée.

accompaniments
Serve this dish with Old-Fashioned Mashed Potatoes (page 68) or Turnip Purée (page 68).

yummy tips
This dish will work just as well with white fish such as cod or sole. In that case, omit the lemon juice, since it tends to overpower the more delicate flavor of white fish.

sole with zucchini and fava beans

sole aux courgettes et aux fèves

10   15   24ʰ   0°

Makes five 3½-ounce (100 g) servings

3 to 4 fillets of sole, around 3½ ounces (100 g) each
3 zucchini, about ⅓ pound (180 g)
About 1 cup (150 g) fava beans, fresh or frozen
1 teaspoon olive oil
½ garlic clove, crushed
2 teaspoons finely chopped shallots

1. Make sure there are no bones in the fish.
2. Wash the zucchini, then cut them into rounds. Shell and peel the fava beans, if using fresh.
3. Heat the olive olive oil in a saucepan over medium heat and brown the garlic and shallots. Add the zucchini and fava beans, cover them halfway with water, and bring to a boil. Cook for about 8 minutes.
4. Place the sole fillets on top of the vegetable mixture, cover, and cook for an additional 2 to 3 minutes.
5. Remove from the heat. When done cooking, 2 to 3 tablespoons of cooking liquid should remain at the bottom of the saucepan. If not, pour some out or add a little water to get the right quantity.
6. Blend until you have a smooth purée.

accompaniments

Serve this dish with Sweet Potato Purée (page 42), Carrot and Cumin Purée (page 67), or Mashed Pumpkin and Apple (page 66).

yummy tips

If you can't find fava beans, replace them with green peas. This recipe can easily be adapted to feed the whole family. Use the ingredients to make a appetizing *parmentier de poisson* (fish pie) with sweet potato topping. Place the zucchini, fava beans, garlic, shallots, a few drops of lemon juice and some basil in a casserole dish. Place the raw sole fillets (allow two to three per person according to their size) on top of the vegetables and cover with a layer of mashed sweet potatoes. Preheat the oven to 400°F (200°C) and bake for 20 minutes. Voilà!

sea bass with fennel and green grapes
bar au fenouil et aux raisins blancs

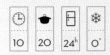

Makes five 3½-ounce (100 g) servings

⅔ fennel bulb, about ⅓ pound (150 g)

Just under ¼ pound (100 g) green grapes, seedless if possible, or about 2 ounces (60 g) of golden raisins

1 carrot, about 2 ounces (60 g)

1 parsnip or 2 fingerling potatoes, about 2 ounces (60 g)

1 sea bass or tilapia fillet, about 3½ ounces (100 g)

1 teaspoon sunflower oil

¾ cup and 2 tablespoons (200 ml) orange juice

1. Wash the fennel, remove the stems, and cut the bulb into thin slices. Slice the grapes in half to remove the seeds, if necessary. Wash and peel the carrot and the parsnip, then dice them.
2. Make sure the sea bass fillet has no bones.
3. In a heavy-bottomed saucepan, heat the oil over medium heat and brown the fennel slices. Add the grapes, carrot, and parsnip. Pour in the orange juice and bring to a boil. Lower the heat, cover, and simmer for 15 minutes.
4. Place the sea bass fillet on top of the vegetables, cover, and cook another 5 or 6 minutes.
5. Remove from heat. When done cooking, about 3 tablespoons of juice should remain. If not, pour some juice out or add a little water to get the right quantity.
6. Blend until you have a smooth purée.

accompaniments
Serve this dish with Carrot Cilantro Purée (page 67) or Sweet Potato Purée (page 42).

yummy tips
For an adult dinner, stuff whole sea bass bellies with fennel and lemon slices. Preheat the oven to 350°F (180°C) and bake for 25 minutes. Serve the fillets over wild rice with fennel and raisins. To prepare the wild rice, brown the fennel slices and the grapes or raisins (preferably golden) in a bit of sunflower oil. Add ½ cup rice (100 g) and stir until the rice is slightly translucent. Add 1¼ cups (300 ml) of water and a pinch of salt. Cover and cook until the water is completely absorbed.

tuna niçoise
thon à la niçoise

10	15	24ʰ	0°

Makes five 3½-ounce (100 g) servings

2 zucchini, about ¼ pound (120 g)
2 tomatoes, just under ½ pound (200 g)
4 slices eggplant, about 2 ounces (60 g)
1 fresh or frozen tuna steak,
about 3½ ounces (100 g)
2 teaspoons olive oil
½ clove garlic, chopped
1 tablespoon tomato paste
½ teaspoon dried thyme
½ cup (120 ml) water

1. Wash the vegetables and cut them into cubes.
2. Cut the tuna into cubes.
3. In a heavy-bottomed saucepan, heat the olive oil over medium heat and brown the garlic and tuna cubes. Add the vegetables, tomato paste, and thyme. Pour in the water and bring to a boil. Lower the heat, cover, and simmer for 15 minutes.
4. Remove from the heat and blend until you have a smooth purée.

accompaniments
This dish goes nicely with Parmesan Polenta (page 69) or Fine Semolina with Thyme (page 69).

yummy tips
If you find the eggplant has added a bitter note to the dish, simply add 1 tablespoon of ketchup—its sugar will neutralize the bitter taste. For a family meal, sear or grill tuna steaks (5 ounces or 150 g per person) until they're pink in the middle (about 4 minutes on each side). Prepare the vegetables with tomato paste, thyme, and ½ cup (120 ml) water according to the recipe and add diced red bell peppers and a pinch of salt. Serve the steaks topped with these mixed vegetables and one of the accompaniments mentioned above.

mashed pumpkin and apple
purée de potiron et de pommes

Makes five 3½-ounce (100 g) servings

Just over 1 pound (500 g) pumpkin
2 sweet-tart apples (Honey Crisp,
Reine des Reinettes),
just under ½ pound (200 g)
1 large fingerling potato
1 scant tablespoon (10 g) butter
2 drops lemon juice

1. Wash and peel the pumpkin, the apples, and the potato. Deseed the pumpkin, remove the apples' cores and any spare seeds, and cut everything into cubes.
2. Put the cubes into a saucepan, cover with water, and bring to a boil. Cook for 15 minutes. Remove from the heat and drain.
3. Blend the cooked fruit and veggies with the butter and lemon juice until you have a smooth purée.

pumpkin purée with cumin
purée de potiron au cumin

Makes five 3½-ounce (100 g) servings

1⅔ pounds pumpkin (750 g)
1 large fingerling potato
1 scant tablespoon (10 g) butter
2 to 3 drops lemon juice
½ to 1 teaspoon ground cumin, to taste

1. Wash and peel the pumpkin and potato. Deseed the pumpkin, and cut the vegetables into small cubes.
2. Put the cubes into a saucepan, cover with water, and bring to a boil. Cook for 15 minutes. Remove from the heat and drain.
3. Blend the vegetables with the butter, lemon juice, and cumin until you have a smooth purée.

carrot and cumin purée
purée de carottes au cumin

5   15

24ʰ   0°

Makes five 3½-ounce
(100 g) servings

6 carrots, about 14 ounces (400 g)
1 teaspoon sunflower oil
1 teaspoon lemon juice
Pinch of ground cumin
½ cup (120 ml) water

1. Wash and peel the carrots, then cut them into rounds.
2. In a heavy-bottomed saucepan, heat the oil and sauté the carrots over medium heat for 5 minutes. Add the lemon juice, cumin, and water. Cook for 10 more minutes. When done, the water should be completely absorbed and the carrots tender.
3. Blend until you have a smooth purée.

carrot cilantro purée
purée de carottes à la coriandre

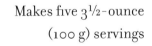

5   15

24ʰ   0°

Makes five 3½-ounce
(100 g) servings

8 carrots, just over 1 pound (500 g)
4 fresh cilantro leaves, chopped
1 teaspoon sunflower oil

1. Wash and peel the carrots, then cut them into rounds.
2. Put the carrots into a saucepan, cover them with water, bring to a boil, and cook for 15 minutes. Remove from the heat and drain.
3. Blend the carrots with the cilantro and sunflower oil until you have a smooth purée.

turnip purée
purée de navets

Makes five 3½-ounce
(100 g) servings

4 turnips, just over 1 pound (500 g)
1 scant tablespoon (10 g) butter

1. Wash and peel the turnips, then cut them into small pieces.
2. Put the turnips into a saucepan, cover them with water, bring to a boil, and cook for 15 minutes. Remove from the heat and drain.
3. Blend the turnips with the butter until you have a smooth purée.

old-fashioned mashed potatoes
purée de pommes de terre à l'ancienne

Makes five 3½-ounce
(100 g) servings

5 large potatoes, about 14 ounces (400 g)
Just under ½ cup (100 ml) milk
1 scant tablespoon (10 g) butter

1. Wash and peel the potatoes, then cut them into small pieces.
2. Put the potatoes into a saucepan, cover them with water, bring to a boil, and cook for 15 minutes. Remove from the heat and drain.
3. Use a potato masher to mash the potatoes with the milk and butter (never blend potatoes, unless you want to make an inedible potato paste).

parmesan polenta
polenta au parmesan

| 1 | 10 |

Makes one 3½-ounce
(100 g) serving

Just under ½ cup (100 ml) milk
2 tablespoons grated Parmesan
1½ tablespoon (10 g) dried polenta

1. Bring the milk to a boil with the Parmesan, stirring constantly over medium heat.
2. Remove from the heat, toss in the polenta, and stir vigorously.
3. Continue to stir until the polenta is creamy and uniform in texture. Serve immediately.

fine semolina with thyme
semoule fine au thym

| 1 | 5 |

Makes one 3½-ounce
(100 g) serving

Just under ¼ cup (60 ml) water
Pinch of dried thyme
3 tablespoons and 1 teaspoon (50 g)
fine semolina

1. Bring the water to a boil with the thyme.
2. Remove the saucepan from the heat and add the semolina. Cover the saucepan and let the semolina expand for 5 minutes.
3. Fluff the semolina with a fork before serving.

fruit coulis
coulis de fruits

Fruit coulis makes a great quick dessert that can be combined with yogurt or soft cheese, depending on what you have in your refrigerator and what Bébé is craving. It's up to you to create your own dessert, mixing and matching the fruit coulis proposed in the following section. And you're not allowed to steal Bébé's dessert!

cherry coulis
coulis de cerises

Makes five 3½-ounce (100 g) servings

1⅓ pounds (600 g) cherries
2 to 3 tablespoons water

1. Wash the cherries and remove the pits.
2. Put the cherries into a saucepan and crush them lightly with your hand or a fork, so they release a bit of their juice. Cook them on low heat for 20 minutes. Add water as needed, if the fruit does not provide enough liquid.
3. Remove from the heat and blend to a smooth coulis.

yummy tips

You and your partner can eat this coulis for dessert on top of a panna cotta or with a slice of aged cheese (such as Comté). Bing cherries are extraordinary in this recipe.

blueberry coulis
coulis de myrtilles

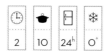

Makes five 3½-ounce (100 g) servings

Just over 1 pound (500 g) blueberries, fresh or frozen
2 to 3 tablespoons water

1. Wash the blueberries.
2. Put the blueberries into a saucepan and crush them lightly with your hand or a fork, so they release a bit of their juice. Cook them over very low heat for 10 minutes. Add water as needed, if the fruit does not provide enough liquid.
3. Remove from the heat and blend to a smooth coulis.

yummy tips

Blueberry stains are very difficult to remove. The little bib Bébé usually wears will not be enough to protect that lovely pullover Grandma gave him! But don't let that danger deprive Bébé of this delicious fruit. Simply dress him in a bigger bib!

raspberry–brown sugar coulis

coulis de framboises et cassonade

2 | 15 | 24ʰ | 0°

Makes five 3½-ounce (100 g) servings

Just over 1 pound (500 g) raspberries, fresh or frozen
1 tablespoon brown sugar
2 tablespoons water (if you're using frozen fruit, don't add water)

1. Wash the raspberries well.
2. Put them into a saucepan and crush them lightly with your hand or a fork, so they release a bit of their juice. Add the brown sugar and water, then cook them over low heat for 15 minutes. If the mixture appears dry to you, add water as needed.
3. Remove from the heat and blend to a smooth coulis.

yummy tips

Raspberries are naturally acidic, which is why this recipe contains a bit of sugar. For bigger kids—and a crunch—you can add the brown sugar at the end of the cooking time. The sugar crystals won't melt and the coulis will be a bit crunchy.

strawberry-mint coulis

coulis de fraises à la menthe

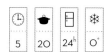

5 | 20 | 24ʰ | 0°

Makes five 3½-ounce (100 g) servings

Just over 1 pound (500 g) strawberries
3 tablespoons water
4 fresh mint leaves

1. Wash the strawberries well and remove any leaves.
2. Put the strawberries into a saucepan and crush them lightly with your hand or a fork, so they release a bit of their juice. Add the water and cook the berries over low heat for 15 minutes.
3. Add the mint leaves and cook for 5 more minutes. If the mixture appears dry to you, add water as needed.
4. Remove from the heat and blend to a smooth coulis.

yummy tips

In early summer, when strawberries are the sweetest, I serve this coulis with vanilla ice cream. I always make extra strawberry coulis and freeze it, so I can take it out in winter and serve it over molten chocolate cake (*fondant au chocolat*).

nectarine coulis
coulis de nectarines

5 | 10 | 24^h | 0°

Makes five 3½-ounce (100 g) servings

8 to 10 nectarines,
just over 1 pound (500 g)
Just under ¼ cup (60 ml) water

1. Peel the nectarines, cut the flesh into pieces, and throw away the pit.
2. Put the nectarine pieces into a saucepan and crush them lightly with your hand or a fork, so they release a bit of their juice. Add the water and cook the nectarines over low heat for 10 minutes. If the mixture appears dry to you, add water as needed.
3. Remove from the heat and blend to a smooth coulis.

yummy tips

Nectarines are easier to peel than peaches, but you can also prepare this coulis with the latter.

mango coulis
coulis de mangue

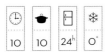

10 | 10 | 24^h | 0°

Makes five 3½-ounce (100 g) servings

3 mangoes, just over 1 pound (500 g)
Just under ¼ cup (60 ml) water

1. Cut off the sides of the mangoes along either side of the pit. Cut the sides into several half-moons and remove the skin. Trim the flesh from around the pits and remove the skin.
2. Put the mango pieces into a saucepan and crush them lightly with your hand or a fork, so they release a bit of their juice. Add the water and cook them over low heat for 10 minutes. If the mixture appears dry to you, add water as needed.
3. Remove from the heat and blend to a smooth coulis.

yummy tips

Having a hard time finding fresh mangoes? Buy frozen instead, perfect for a coulis and cheaper than fresh.

raw, pulpy, and blended fruits
les crus, pulpes et mixes

All of the following fruits can be blended or crushed raw and served to Bébé. It's best to prepare and serve them on the spot, since they contain too much water to withstand the freezing process. Serve them with yogurt or, if Bébé has learned to chew, a soft cake or cookie.

Once Bébé has acquired a taste for raw fruit and has her first teeth, feel free to serve her these raw fruits in large pieces that she can eat with her own fingers.

melon
Cut the melon into slices and remove the skin and seeds. Blend.

peach
Cut the flesh from the pit and, using a knife, take the skin off the flesh. Blend.

mango
Cut off the sides of the mango along either side of the pit. Cut these sides into several half-moons and remove the skin. Trim the flesh from around the pit and remove the skin. Blend.

watermelon
Cut the melon into pieces and remove the rind and seeds. Blend.

clementine pulp with a hint of cinnamon
Peel the clementine and divide it into segments. Using a knife, cut each segment lengthwise and separate the pulp from the thin skin. Remove any seeds. Crush the pulp with a fork. Do not blend, unless you want juice! Mix in a dash of cinnamon.

orange pulp with a drop of orange blossom water
Peel the orange and divide it into segments. Using a knife, cut each segment lengthwise and separate the pulp from the thin skin. Remove any seeds. Crush the pulp with a fork. Do not blend, unless you want juice. Add a drop of orange blossom water and mix well.

Vera, 16 months, foodie

first dinners

9 months+

First Dinners

Dr. Jean Lalau Keraly, Pediatric Nutritionist and Endocrinologist

At nine months, your little one is no longer a baby but not a big kid, either. At this age, he can discover real dishes composed of vegetables and starches. Even though the list of foods he can eat has gotten longer, you still need to feed him sensibly, without pressure to grow up too quickly. His body is still fragile, and there will be plenty of time for him to try Aunt Petra's sauerkraut later, when his stomach is able to digest it properly.

choose foods wisely

Now you'll be preparing dinner based on foods kids tend to love: rice, pasta, polenta. These starches do a suitable job satisfying a baby's stomach, ensuring he'll have a good night's sleep and won't be awakened by hunger pains.

small bites

It's also at this age that your little gourmet is introduced to chunky food. No more smooth purées: You'll gradually introduce ones with coarsely chopped pieces that can be mashed. His meals are starting to look more and more like your own!

just like grown-ups

Now that he is sitting up straight and having fun gnawing on his crust of bread, why not invite him to the family dinner table? By integrating Baby naturally into your dinners, you're teaching him to see a meal as a moment to relax and share, a pleasurable time when he can interact with the family and taste the grown-up dishes, as long as they don't pose any danger (allergies or intolerances).

ambience is everything

If your little one gets into the habit of eating dinner in a hurry, with the television going full blast and the family getting all worked up as dinnertime approaches, it's guaranteed his appetite or enthusiasm will reflect that. The pleasure of eating comes not only from the food itself, but from the atmosphere in which it is consumed.

a bit of advice

If you can't be there for Baby's dinner—on a regular or an occasional basis—avoid making a big entrance if you happen to arrive home during his dinnertime. He's missed you so much during the long day that his attention will inevitably be focused on you. This is enough to make him push aside even the tastiest dishes in the world! So let him eat peacefully and come say hello once he's had his dinner. Then you'll have plenty of time to hold and pamper him, knowing that he's been well fed. Finally, make sure you don't tuck your baby into bed immediately after he's eaten. Would you like to go to bed after a good dish of risotto? Too heavy! Spend about an hour interacting and cuddling with him, preparing him for bedtime.

recipes with infinite (or almost infinite) combinations . . .

Nothing's better than diversity for expanding Bébé's palate. For this reason, I've separated the main dishes from their accompaniments (listed under *avec . . .*) so you can change up the recipes on a whim. Try them with my suggestions or try out your own recipe combinations. Bébé will discover, to his delight, that he can enjoy Risotto Milanese *avec* Crushed Tomatoes *ou* Creamy Spinach. You can choose what to serve when, according to the season, the mood of the chef, or the suggestions of your *petit gourmet*!

risotto milanese
risotto milanais

| 5 | 20 | 24ʰ | 0˚ |

Makes five 3½-ounce (100 g) servings

1 tablespoon olive oil
2 teaspoons finely chopped shallots
¾ cup (150 g) round rice (Arborio is perfect)
¼ cup (60 ml) vegetable stock
2 cups (500 ml) water
Just under ½ cup (100 g) grated Parmesan
1 tablespoon crème fraîche

1. In a heavy-bottomed saucepan, heat the olive oil over medium heat and brown the shallots.
2. Add the rice. Stir and cook for several minutes, until the rice is mostly translucent.
3. Add the vegetable stock and half of the water and bring to a boil. Lower the heat and cook for 7 minutes, stirring regularly.
4. Gradually add the rest of the water and continue cooking, stirring regularly, until the rice is tender, about 10 minutes.
5. Remove from heat, add the Parmesan and the crème fraîche, and stir. The risotto should be smooth and creamy. If it is dry, add a few tablespoons of hot water and stir until you reach desired consistency.

yummy tips

To entertain Bébé, empty out a beefsteak tomato and serve the risotto inside it. Guaranteed success! This is how Maya learned to appreciate fresh tomatoes, since she loved eating her "bowl!"

This risotto is just as good for grown-ups as it is for kids. When I eat with my children, I simply add a pinch of salt and serve it alongside a roasted chicken breast with lemon.

avec . . . crushed tomatoes and carrots

concassé de tomates et carottes

10 | 15 | 24ʰ | 0°

Makes five 3½-ounce (100 g) servings

3 tomatoes, about 14 ounces (400 g)
4 carrots, about ½ pound (250 g)
1 teaspoon olive oil
½ garlic clove, finely chopped
4 to 5 basil leaves

1. Wash the vegetables. Cut the tomatoes into quarters. Peel the carrots and cut them into thin rounds.
2. In a heavy-bottomed saucepan, heat the olive oil over medium heat and brown the garlic. Add the vegetables, lower the heat, cover, and simmer for 10 to 12 minutes. Do not add water: The tomatoes should provide enough liquid, as long as the heat is kept low. Add the basil leaves and cook for 3 more minutes.
3. Remove from the heat and blend the mixture until you have a texture that's somewhere between chopped and mashed, depending on Bébé's preference.

yummy tips

Though I prefer to serve the risotto and the crushed tomatoes and carrots side by side (to better appreciate their flavors), they also happen to taste great combined.

avec . . . butternut squash with sage

potimarron et à la sauge

10   15   24ʰ   0°

Makes five 3½-ounce (100 g) servings

1 large slice butternut squash, just over 1 pound (500 g)
2 teaspoons olive oil
3 to 4 fresh sage leaves, finely chopped

1. Preheat the oven to 400°F (200°C).
2. Remove the squash skin and seeds, and dice the flesh into small cubes.
3. Spread the squash cubes on a baking sheet covered with aluminum foil and coat the cubes with the olive oil.
4. Bake in the middle of the oven for 15 minutes, until the squash is tender and begins to brown.
5. Remove the baking sheet from the oven and add the sage. Lightly crush the squash pieces with a fork before serving.

yummy tips

Can't find butternut squash? If you're looking for an alternative, carrots are better than pumpkin, since the latter contains too much water for this recipe. When using carrots, cut them into small cubes and boil them in water for 15 minutes instead of baking. When Maya was a bit older, she loved this mixed with Risotto Milanese (page 80) using half carrots, half corn, and lots of sage.

fine semolina with orange
semoule fine à l'orange

⏰	🍲	🗄	❄
1	5	24ʰ	0˙

Makes one 3½-ounce (100 g) serving

Just under ⅓ cup (70 ml) orange juice
3 tablespoons and 1 teaspoon (50 g) fine semolina

1. In a saucepan, bring the orange juice to a boil.
2. Remove the saucepan from the heat, add the semolina, and stir. Cover and let the semolina expand for 5 minutes.
3. Fluff the semolina with a fork before serving.

yummy tips

Is the semolina too dry on its own? If so, after the semolina expands, mix in more orange juice (up to just under ½ cup [100 ml] total) and 2 heaping tablespoons of Carrot Purée (page 36) to moisten it. If you serve it this way, you can easily prepare several servings in advance and freeze them.

avec . . . vegetable tagine

un tajine de légumes

| 10 | 20 | 24ʰ | 0' |

Makes five 3½-ounce (100 g) servings

2 zucchini, about ¼ pound (120 g)
2 carrots, just under ¼ pound (100 g)
2 tomatoes, just under ½ pound (200 g)
4 slices eggplant, about 2 ounces (60 g)
4 dried apricots
2 teaspoons olive oil
½ garlic clove, chopped
Pinch of ground ginger
Pinch of ground cumin
Pinch of finely chopped fresh cilantro
1 tablespoon tomato paste
Just under ½ cup (100 ml) water

1. Wash the vegetables. Peel the carrots and cut all the vegetables into cubes. Chop the dried apricots.
2. In a heavy-bottomed saucepan, heat the olive oil over medium heat and brown the garlic. Add the spices and cilantro and the apricots. Cook for 1 minute, stirring regularly. Add the vegetables, tomato paste, and water. Bring to a boil. Lower the heat, cover, and simmer over low heat for 15 minutes.
3. Remove the saucepan from heat and blend the mixture until smooth.

yummy tips

You can start small and increase the quantity of spices in this recipe bit by bit until Bébé gets used to them. The first time you make this tagine, replace the ginger with 2 to 3 drops of lemon juice and add just a touch of cumin.

avec . . . ratatouille
une ratatouille

🕐	🍲	🧊	❄
10	15	24ʰ	0˙

Makes five 3½-ounce (100 g) servings

3 zucchini, about ⅓ pound (180 g)
2 tomatoes, just under ½ pound (250 g)
½ pound eggplant (250 g)
2 teaspoons olive oil
½ garlic clove, chopped
2 teaspoons finely chopped shallots
1 tablespoon tomato paste
Pinch of dried thyme
Just under ½ cup (100 ml) water

1. Wash the vegetables and cut them into medium-size cubes.
2. In a heavy saucepan, heat the olive oil over medium heat and sauté the garlic and shallots until golden. Add the vegetables, tomato paste, and thyme. Add the water and bring to a boil. Cover and simmer over low heat for 15 minutes.
3. Remove from heat and blend to obtain a coarse texture.

yummy tips

For a luxurious take on this recipe, use cherry tomatoes instead of large ones. Add them whole so they release their juices slowly and don't overcook. If you freeze one portion of this recipe, you'll be one step ahead when you want to make Tuna Niçoise with Thyme Semolina (page 110).

pasta shapes with soft cheese and basil
petites pâtes au fromage à tartiner et au basilic

1   8   24ʰ   0˚

Makes one 3½-ounce (100 g) serving

A heaping ⅓ cup (100 g) small pasta shapes (such as mini-macaroni or alphabet shapes)
1 wedge or rounded teaspoon soft cheese, such as Laughing Cow
4 to 5 fresh basil leaves, finely chopped

1. Cook the pasta according to the package instructions, with a pinch of salt.
2. Drain and return to the pan.
3. Add the cheese and basil, and stir. Remove from the heat as soon as the cheese has melted.

yummy tips

Choose whole wheat or spelt pasta, both which have a high nutritional value and a pleasant nutty taste. Richer in fiber than traditional pasta, they also aid in digestion.

ROSEO

avec . . . primavera sauce

une sauce primavera

⏰	🍲	🗄	❄
10	15	24ʰ	0°

Makes five 3½-ounce (100 g) servings

2 zucchini, about ¼ pound (120 g)
1½ cups (100 g) broccoli florets
⅔ cup (100 g) green beans
2 teaspoons olive oil
2 teaspoons finely chopped shallots
A heaping ½ cup (100 g) peas,
fresh or frozen
½ cup (120 ml) vegetable stock
3 tablespoons crème fraîche

1. Wash the zucchini and broccoli and cut them into small pieces. Trim the ends of the green beans and cut them into quarters.
2. In a heavy-bottomed saucepan, heat the olive oil over medium heat and cook the shallots until golden. Add the zucchini, broccoli, green beans, peas, vegetable stock, and if necessary, enough water to cover the vegetables halfway. Bring to a boil, then lower the heat, cover, and cook for 10 minutes.
3. Drain the vegetables, setting aside about 3 tablespoons of the cooking liquid. Return the vegetables to the pan, add the crème fraîche, and reheat the mixture with some of the reserved liquid.
4. Blend to a coarse purée. Adjust the texture with the reserved cooking liquid, if necessary.

yummy tips

You can speed up this recipe by using frozen vegetables, since they are precut and washed. If you decide to serve this sauce over Pasta Shapes with Soft Cheese and Basil (page 88), opt for light crème fraîche so the sauce doesn't turn out too rich.

avec . . . fresh tomato sauce
une sauce aux tomates fraîches

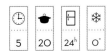

⏱	☗	▯	❄
5	20	24ʰ	0˚

Makes five 3½-ounce (100 g) servings

5 tomatoes, about 1⅓ pounds (600 g)
2 teaspoons olive oil
½ garlic clove, finely chopped

1. Wash the tomatoes and cut them into quarters.
2. In a heavy-bottomed saucepan, heat the olive oil over medium-high heat and cook the garlic until golden.
3. Add the tomatoes, reduce the heat, cover, and cook over medium heat for 15 to 20 minutes (depending on the size of the tomatoes).
4. Remove from the heat and blend to a coarse purée.

yummy tips

I like to make this recipe with cherry tomatoes, which are slightly sweeter than their larger counterparts. (It may be decadent, but hey, we'll tell Dr. Lalau Keraly not to read this tip!) If you find the tomatoes too acidic, add 1 tablespoon of ketchup to the sauce.

avec . . . creamy spinach
épinards à la crème

5   12   24ʰ   0ˮ

Makes five 3½-ounce (100 g) servings

3⅓ cups (500 g) frozen spinach
½ cup (120 ml) vegetable stock
2 tablespoons crème fraîche

1. Put the frozen spinach into a saucepan. Add the vegetable stock and, if necessary, enough water to cover. Cover and bring to a boil.
2. Reduce the heat to medium and cook for 10 minutes.
3. Drain thoroughly: Spinach retains plenty of water. Add the crème fraîche and return to the saucepan to heat through.
4. Blend until you have a coarse purée.

yummy tips

Served with pasta, this recipe may at first seem like an unusual combination. But trust me, it's simply delicious. The slightly acidic notes in both the spinach and the crème fraîche are marvelous with all kinds of pasta. When I eat with the kids, I roast a salmon fillet in the oven to go along with this dish.

avec . . . fava beans, ricotta and basil

fèves à la ricotta et au basilic

5   15   24ʰ   0°

Makes five 3½-ounce (100 g) servings

1 zucchini, about 2 ounces (60 g)
About 4 cups (400 g) fava beans, frozen
½ cup (120 ml) vegetable stock
2 tablespoons ricotta
4 to 5 fresh basil leaves, finely chopped

1. Wash the zucchini and cut it into small pieces.
2. Put the fava beans into a saucepan, add the vegetable stock and enough water to cover. Cover and bring to a boil. Lower the heat to medium and cook for 10 minutes. Add the zucchini and cook for another 5 minutes.
3. Drain, leaving about 3 tablespoons of cooking liquid in the pan.
4. Mix the vegetables with the remaining liquid, the ricotta, and the basil.

yummy tips

If you can't find ricotta, use fresh goat cheese. This recipe pairs well with Pasta Shapes with Soft Cheese and Basil (page 88), but then you should omit the soft cheese.

braised green lentils and spinach
étuvée de lentilles vertes et épinards

⊕	♨	▤	❄
5	30	24ʰ	0°

Makes five 5-ounce (150 g) servings

1 cup (200 g) green lentils
2 cups (300 g) frozen spinach
½ cup (120 ml) vegetable stock

1. Rinse the lentils, picking over them and discarding any stones or debris.
2. Put the lentils into a saucepan and cover them with twice their volume of water. Bring to a boil, reduce the heat, cover, and cook over medium heat for 30 minutes, or until the lentils are tender.
3. While the lentils are cooking, cook the spinach in the vegetable stock in another saucepan over medium heat for 10 minutes.
4. Remove the spinach from heat, drain, and give it a quick stir.
5. Drain the lentils and mix in the spinach.

accompaniments
Serve with basmati rice or bread topped with fresh soft cheese.

yummy tips
When the grown-ups sit down to dinner with the kids, I serve this dish along with a roasted cod fillet enhanced with a few drops of fresh lemon juice.

pumpkin, sweet potato, and vanilla soup
velouté de potiron et de patates douces à la vanille

10 20 24ʰ 0˚

Makes five 7-ounce (200 g) servings

*1 large slice pumpkin,
about ⅔ pound (300 g)*
2 sweet potatoes, about 1 pound (450 g)
1 cup (240 ml) vegetable stock
Just under 3 cups (700 ml) water
1 vanilla bean
2 tablespoons crème fraîche
2 teaspoons lemon juice

1. Peel and deseed the pumpkin and cut the flesh into pieces.
2. Wash and peel the sweet potatoes and cut them into cubes.
3. Put the vegetables into a large saucepan. Add the vegetable stock and the water. With a knife, open the vanilla bean lengthwise and scrape the seeds into the pan. Add the bean to the pan.
4. Bring the mixture to a boil. Cover and cook over medium heat for 20 minutes.
5. Remove from the heat and remove the vanilla bean.
6. Add the crème fraîche and lemon juice and blend until smooth.
7. The soup should be creamy. If it is too thick, simply add some water. If it is too wet, boil some additional sweet potato or potato, add to the mixture, and blend again.

yummy tips

The flavors in this soup offer an excellent opportunity to introduce Bébé to mushrooms. When Maya was little, I used to chop some mushrooms and sauté them in a bit of butter before placing them on top of the soup. She loved them! Nowadays, she happily chomps on raw mushrooms.

broccoli and cheese soup

soupe aux brocolis et au fromage à tartiner

5   10   24ʰ   0°

Makes five 7-ounce (200 g) servings

6 cups (400 g) broccoli florets
1 teaspoon olive oil
2 teaspoons finely chopped shallots
1 cup (240 ml) vegetable stock
Just under 3 cups (700 ml) water
4 wedges or rounded teaspoons soft cheese, such as Laughing Cow

1. Wash the broccoli and cut into small pieces.
2. In a heavy-bottomed saucepan, heat the olive oil over medium-high heat and cook the shallots for 1 minute, or until translucent. Add the vegetable stock, water, and broccoli and bring to a boil. Reduce the heat, cover, and cook for 10 minutes.
3. Remove from the heat, add the soft cheese, and blend until smooth.
4. The soup should be creamy. If it is too thick, add a little water. If it is too wet, boil some broccoli florets, add them to the soup, and blend again.

accompaniments

Serve with a bit of fresh bread, if Bébé likes it.

yummy tips

For babies over twelve months, liven up this soup with a bit of ground nutmeg. You can also try leaving a few whole broccoli florets in the middle of the soup, to give those new teeth something to crunch on!

cream of corn and tomatoes

crème de maïs et tomates

| 5 | 15 | 24ʰ | 0° |

Makes five 7-ounce (200 g) servings

2 tomatoes, about ½ pound (250 g)
1¾ cups (300 g) corn, frozen or canned
4 fresh sage leaves, chopped
1 cup (240 ml) vegetable stock
Just under 3 cups (700 ml) water
2 tablespoons crème fraîche

1. Wash the tomatoes and cut them into quarters.
2. Put the corn, tomatoes, and sage into a big saucepan, add the vegetable stock and water, and bring to a boil. Cover and cook over medium heat for 15 minutes.
3. Remove from the heat, add the crème fraîche, and blend until smooth.
4. The soup should be creamy. If it is too thick, add a little water. If it is too wet, add some corn directly to the mixture, cook for an additional 5 to 7 minutes, and blend again.

yummy tips

Your "big baby" will probably be delighted to crunch on a few whole corn kernels, so leave a few in the soup!

Chiara, 20 months, official taster

first big-kid lunches

&

big-kid dinners with the family

12 months+

Big-Kid Lunches, Big-Kid Dinners

Dr. Jean Lalau Keraly, Pediatric Nutritionist and Endocrinologist

One year old already! Your little one has sprouted up at the speed of light, thanks largely to the good meals you've lovingly prepared for her. After some occasionally laborious weeks of gradually introducing new foods, her twelve-month-old body is able to digest big-kid food. The list of forbidden foods is dwindling (except for those who have been diagnosed with allergies). Your baby can now sit at the family table and share meals with her parents and brothers or sisters, with textures adapted to her needs.

baby teeth

At twelve months, not all babies are in fact equal: Those cutting their baby teeth are able to consume increasingly bigger chunks. Others boast a wide, toothless smile and are still in the mashed—or even smooth purée—phase. Don't panic: Each baby has her own rhythm. As the first baby teeth appear, the transition to "biting" her food will take place naturally. It's up to you to adapt and progressively guide your little one to appreciate meals that have more texture.

slightly bigger bites

Limiting your baby to exclusively smooth foods is truly depriving her of the richness of flavors that bits of meat, vegetables, and fruits can add to her diet. Doing so keeps her in a "baby" stage, which will eventually damage her development of motor skills and her rapport with a normal diet. No need to hurry, which will only frighten and upset her. Simply keep in mind that when your child is older than eighteen months, it's recommended to proceed to dishes with substantial chunks.

holding her own baby spoon

This is around the time that Baby will gradually free herself from her parents' assistance with feeding. It's not easy eating a smooth, liquid purée on her own. But what fun it is for her to pick up chunks of tender zucchini and put them into her own mouth! Experiencing this kind of freedom is what's important at your toddler's developmental stage. The more independent she becomes, the better your chances to march her down the path to healthy eating. Not only is she acquiring an autonomy that will be useful in her general development, she's also taking charge of her own diet. She's becoming an actor, not just a spectator. Baby is growing up!

but be careful!

Though Baby's diet will resemble the rest of the family's from now on, it doesn't mean you should let her pick up the family's bad eating habits. After months of paying scrupulous attention to expanding their baby's food horizons, parents tend to lose steam by the time their little one has blown out her first birthday candles, and they gradually invest less time in preparing her meals. So baby meals tend to become an exact copy of the family's, which means they become more simplified and less varied—with fewer fruits and vegetables and too much salt and protein.

a balanced diet

Obviously, you will not make this error. If Baby can now eat as you do, it's the right time to pass on the good habits you've established during your little one's initiation to taste—but this time you should also pass them on to the rest of the family. In summary, good habits include lots of vegetables, fruits, whole-grain cereals, fresh herbs, a little protein, fewer bad fats, and fewer sugars. It doesn't mean you're going to put the whole family on a diet! Throughout this book, you've noticed that eating well doesn't go hand in hand with eating low-fat, bland foods. So offer your baby well-balanced recipes without too much protein (up to age two, no more than 1½ ounces/40 g of meat or fish daily) and an important supply of iron and calcium. Also don't forget that your big kid, at this age, no longer needs a snack between breakfast and lunch—snacking increases the risk of childhood obesity—nor a bottle of milk during the night.

in this chapter

In this chapter dedicated to our big kids, you'll find savory and sweet recipes that take into account pediatric recommendations and the pressures of modern parenting, along with the desires of your budding gastronome, who is starting to know and identify her favorite dishes. You're not about to complain, since it was you who launched the taste initiation in the first place. It is finally time for her to gently take the lead vis-à-vis her culinary preferences. It's by considering food a source of pleasure and discovery, and not of stress or obligation, that your baby will continue to navigate along the path of (good) taste.

something's cooking!

Introducing Bébé to gastronomy is not about being tied down to the home-cooked dishes we loved as children—our elbows on the dinner table, impatiently waiting for Grandma's steaming ladle to fill our desperately empty bowl. Keeping in mind that our grandmothers' tried-and-true recipes were not always completely focused on the nutritional needs of our littlest ones, I made adjustments to them, taking inspiration from the best aspects of the previous generation's incomparable cuisine. So in these pages you'll find one-pot meals specifically designed for kids ages one and up and bursting with vitamins and flavor. And, just between us, if you want to double or triple the recipe for the whole family's enjoyment, that's allowed, too.

chicken and vegetables in coconut milk
poulet au lait de coco et petits legumes

15   20   24ʰ   0°

Makes five 4¼-ounce (120 g) servings

2 carrots, just under ¼ pound (100 g)
1 zucchini, about 2 ounces (60 g)
⅔ cup (100 g) green beans
5 to 6 broccoli florets
1 chicken breast, about 3½ ounces (100 g)
1 tablespoon sunflower oil
1 garlic clove, finely chopped
½ teaspoon ground ginger
3 to 4 fresh cilantro leaves, chopped
¾ cup and 2 tablespoons (200 ml) coconut milk
1 tablespoon lemon juice
Pinch each of salt and brown sugar
Just under ½ cup (100 ml) water

1. Wash the vegetables and peel the carrots. Cut the zucchini and carrots into rounds. Trim the green beans and cut them into pieces. Roughly chop the broccoli florets. Cut the chicken breast into pieces.
2. Heat the sunflower oil over medium heat in a large heavy-bottomed saucepan and cook the chicken pieces until golden brown.
3. Add the garlic, ginger, and cilantro, and continue cooking for 1 minute, without browning too much.
4. Add the vegetables, coconut milk, lemon juice, salt, brown sugar, and water and bring to a boil. Cover and simmer over low heat for 15 minutes.
5. Remove from the heat, add the cilantro, and blend until you have a coarse purée.

accompaniments
Serve with basmati rice. For one portion, boil just under ½ cup (100 ml) water in a saucepan. Add just under ¼ cup (50 g) rice, cover, and cook over low heat for 15 minutes, or until the water is completely absorbed.

yummy tips
Is Bébé not wild about coconut milk? Replace it with crème fraîche and leave out the lemon juice. The crème fraîche already has the slightly acidic note this dish calls for.

chicken tagine with raisins

tajine de poulet aux raisins secs

Makes five 4¼-ounce
(120 g) servings

5 carrots, about ¾ pound (330 g)
1 zucchini, about 2 ounces (60 g)
2 tomatoes, just under ½ pound (200 g)
1 tablespoon olive oil
1 chicken thigh, about ½ pound (220 g)
1 onion, finely chopped
1 garlic clove, finely chopped
Pinch of salt
½ teaspoon ground ginger
½ teaspoon ground allspice
1 tablespoon raisins (preferably golden)
¾ cup and 2 tablespoons (200 ml)
orange juice
Just under ½ cup (100 ml) water

1. Wash the vegetables and peel the carrots. Cut the carrots and the zucchini into rounds and cut the tomatoes into quarters.
2. Heat the olive oil in a large, heavy-bottomed saucepan over medium heat and brown the chicken thigh (skin-side down). Add the onion, garlic, salt, and spices and continue cooking for another minute, without browning too much.
3. Add the vegetables, half the raisins, the orange juice, and water. Cover and let simmer over low heat for 15 minutes. Add the other half of the raisins and cook for 10 more minutes.
4. Remove from the heat and take out the chicken thigh. Remove the bones and skin. Put the meat back into the mixture and blend roughly until you have a coarse purée.

accompaniments
Serve this tagine with Fine Semolina with Thyme (page 69).

yummy tips
For bigger kids, prepare this dish through step 3 with chicken drumsticks. Perfect for eating with their fingers!

lamb tagine with apricots
tajine d'agneau aux abricots secs

10	30	24ʰ	0°

Makes five 4¼-ounce (120 g) servings

4 carrots, about ½ pound (250 g)
2 zucchini, about ¼ pound (120 g)
2 tomatoes, just under ½ pound (200 g)
3½ ounces (100 g) leg of lamb
(or shoulder)
1 tablespoon olive oil
1 garlic clove, finely chopped
Pinch of salt
½ teaspoon ground ginger
½ teaspoon ground allspice
10 dried apricots

1. Wash the vegetables and peel the carrots. Cut the carrots and zucchini into rounds and cut the tomatoes into quarters. Trim the fat from the lamb and cut it into pieces.
2. Heat the olive oil in a large heavy-bottomed saucepan over medium heat and brown the lamb pieces on all sides. Add the garlic, salt, and spices and cook for another minute, without browning too much.
3. Add the vegetables and half the dried apricots, and cover them halfway with water. Bring to a boil, cover, and simmer over low heat for 15 minutes. Add the rest of the apricots and continue cooking for 10 more minutes.
4. Remove from the heat and blend roughly until you have a coarse purée.

accompaniments
Serve this tagine with Fine Semolina with Thyme (page 69) or Fine Semolina with Orange (page 84).

yummy tips
For grown-ups, this tagine needs more zing! Liven it up with a dash of hot sauce or cayenne pepper. For crunchiness, add a handful of blanched almonds to the mixture just after cooking. Sprinkle a bit of cinnamon over the semolina.

italian meatballs
boulettes de viande comme en Italie

20	25	24ʰ	0°

Makes five 4¼-ounce (120 g) servings

For the meatballs
3½ ounces (100 g) ground beef
½ onion, finely chopped
1 potato, cooked and mashed
Pinch of salt
Freshly ground pepper to taste

For the tomato sauce
2 tomatoes, just under ½ pound (200 g)
2 teaspoons olive oil
1 teaspoon finely chopped garlic
1 tablespoon tomato paste
4 fresh basil leaves, chopped

1. Mix together the ground beef, onion, mashed potato, salt, and pepper. Make small balls (about 15) and let sit for 10 to 15 minutes at room temperature.
2. Wash the tomatoes and cut them into quarters.
3. In a heavy-bottomed saucepan, heat half of the olive oil over medium heat and cook the garlic until lightly golden but not brown. Add the tomatoes, tomato paste, and basil. Cover and simmer for 10 minutes.
4. Heat the rest of the olive oil in another pan over medium heat and carefully add the meatballs. Brown them on all sides so that they are sealed, meaning you can no longer see any raw meat on the outside.
5. Remove the tomato sauce from the heat and blend. Add the meatballs and cook over low heat, for about 10 minutes, or until the meatballs are cooked through.

accompaniments
Serve these meatballs with cooked pasta shapes sprinkled with a bit of grated Parmesan.

yummy tips
Sometimes I find it too laborious and time-consuming to make my own meatballs, so I often use frozen mini meatballs. Heating them up in the tomato sauce takes 10 minutes and couldn't be easier!

baby beef bourguignon
boeuf bourguignon spécial bébé

10 30 24ʰ 0°

Makes five 4¼-ounce
(120 g) servings

4 carrots, about ½ pound (250 g)
2 zucchini, about ¼ pound (120 g)
2 tomatoes, just under ½ pound (200 g)
3½ ounces (100 g) rump/chuck roast or
other slow-cooking beef
2 teaspoons olive oil
½ onion, finely chopped
2 slices of bacon or dry ham
1 tablespoon tomato paste
½ teaspoon dried thyme
Freshly ground pepper to taste
1 bay leaf

1. Wash vegetables and peel the carrots. Cut the carrots and zucchini into rounds and cut the tomatoes into quarters. Cut the beef into pieces.
2. In a heavy-bottomed saucepan, heat the olive oil over medium heat. Brown the beef pieces on all sides. Add the onions and bacon and continue to cook for 1 minute without browning too much.
3. Add vegetables, tomato paste, thyme, pepper, and bay leaf, and cover halfway with water. Bring to a boil, cover, and simmer over low heat for 25 minutes.
4. Remove from the heat, take out the bay leaf, and blend until you have a coarse purée.

accompaniments
This bourguignon is well paired with Old-Fashioned Mashed Potatoes (page 68).

yummy tips
I top this dish off with caramelized chestnuts. They're Maya's favorite—and super-easy to prepare! Buy vacuum-packed chestnuts. In a skillet, melt a pat of butter over low heat and gently sauté the chestnuts with a generous pinch of brown sugar (or white sugar if that's all you have). Turn the chestnuts constantly, until the sugar melts and the chestnuts are good and hot.

express lunches for busy days

In our hectic lives as overactive parents, we can't always spend half an hour in front of the stove simmering, braising, chopping, and elaborating inventive recipes. Between the shopping (not to mention unloading and putting away the groceries), the picking up at school, and the getting to the pediatrician on time, your schedule is starting to make the president's look like a summer-camp counselor's! With this shortage of time in mind, I created a handful of "express recipes"—ready in the blink of an eye but still just as appetizing and nutrition-rich as the others in this book. Who's getting a gold star?

tuna niçoise with thyme semolina
thon à la niçoise et semoule fine au thym

⏱	🍲	🗄	❄
2	5	24ʰ	0°

Makes one 4¼-ounce (120 g) serving

3½ ounces (100 g) ratatouille (which you wisely froze the last time you made it—see page 87)
About 1 ounce (30 g) canned tuna in water
¼ cup (60 ml) water
½ teaspoon dried thyme
Pinch of salt
3 tablespoons and 1 teaspoon (50 g) fine semolina

1. Heat the ratatouille in a saucepan over medium heat.
2. Drain the tuna and fluff it with a fork.
3. Mix the tuna into the ratatouille, reduce the heat, and let cook for 5 minutes.
4. Meanwhile, bring the water to a boil. Add the thyme, salt, and the semolina. Cover and let sit for 5 minutes (giving the semolina time to expand).
5. Fluff the semolina with a fork and serve with the tuna niçoise.

yummy tips

This dish can also be made with Fresh Tomato Sauce (page 91), which you have (of course) prepared in advance and can therefore pop out of your freezer whenever you need it!

pasta with ham and peas
pâtes au jambon blanc et petits pois

2 5 24ʰ 0˙

Makes one 4¼-ounce (120 g) serving

A heaping ⅓ cup (100 g) pasta shapes
A heaping ¼ cup (50 g) peas,
fresh or frozen
1 scant tablespoon (10 g) butter
1 teaspoon finely chopped shallots
1 slice ham, cut into bite-size pieces
2 tablespoons crème fraîche

1. Cook the pasta according to the package instructions.
2. Meanwhile, bring a small saucepan of water to a boil, add the peas, and cook for 5 minutes. Drain and put them back into the pan.
3. Return the pan to the heat and add the butter, shallots, and ham. Cook for 1 to 2 minutes, stirring constantly.
4. Add the crème fraîche and bring to a boil, then remove from the heat.
5. Drain the pasta. Serve topped with the ham-and-pea sauce.

yummy tips

To speed up recipes like this one, I always keep a supply of finely chopped shallots, garlic, and onions in my freezer. If you have them handy, you won't even need a cutting board to make this simple pasta dish.

chicken with broccoli and basmati rice
poulet aux brocolis et riz basmati

5 | 10

Makes one 4¼-ounce (120 g) serving

1 cup (240 ml) water
About ¼ cup (50 g) basmati rice
1 teaspoon olive oil
1 teaspoon finely chopped shallots
About 1 ounce (30 g) chicken breast, cut into small pieces
¾ cup (50 g) broccoli florets
2 tablespoons crème fraîche
1 tablespoon grated Parmesan

1. Bring half of the water to a boil in a saucepan with the rice and a pinch of salt. Reduce the heat, cover, and cook for 10 minutes, or until the water is completely absorbed.
2. In a heavy-bottomed pan, heat the olive oil, add the shallots, and cook for 1 minute.
3. Add the chicken pieces and brown them on all sides. Add the remaining water and the broccoli florets. Cook, uncovered, for 7 more minutes.
4. Add the crème fraîche and the Parmesan. Simmer for 2 to 3 minutes. Serve with the rice.

yummy tips
This dish can be made with all kinds of white meat: chicken, turkey, veal, and even pork. Use whatever you have. I don't recommend using a lighter cheese than Parmesan—the chicken and broccoli benefit from its saltiness.

now I can eat like everyone else

It's here! The moment all parent chefs eagerly await: when Bébé can eat like the rest of the family. At one year, he's ready to take that step. You can finally stop dividing your brain into two—or even three—parts in order to juggle the daily menus for Bébé, Little Brother, Big Sister, and the grown-ups. In these pages, you'll find recipes suited for little and big palates! The difference that remains, above all, is what is done to the food after it's prepared. You'll serve the dish as is to the older family members and adjust the preparation (that is, its texture) to fit Bébé's needs: slices if he likes eating those or coarsely blended if he prefers smoother meals. But with these recipes, sharing is the name of the game. Everyone can enjoy themselves around the table with the same yummy dish. For Bébé, taking full part in this ritual is a precious moment in his gustatory learning process. Enjoy the family meal!

turkey cutlet with prosciutto, sweet potato purée and peas

escalope de dinde au jambon de parme, purée de patates douces et petits pois

10   15   24ʰ   0°

Makes 2 adult portions and 1 baby portion

2 sweet potatoes, about 1 pound (450 g)
2 turkey cutlets,
about 5 ounces (150 g) each
2½ slices prosciutto
1¼ cups (200 g) peas, fresh or frozen
1 scant tablespoon (10 g) butter

1. Wash and peel the sweet potatoes. Cut them into cubes.
2. Put the sweet potato cubes into a saucepan and cover with water. Bring to a boil, lower the heat, and simmer for 15 minutes.
3. Preheat the oven to 400°F (200°C).
4. Cut a thin slice off one of the cutlets for Bébé. Roll the cutlets inside a slice of ham each. Then roll the slice of cutlet inside the ½ slice of ham.
5. Put the turkey cutlets onto a baking sheet covered with aluminum foil. Bake the grown-ups' cutlets for 10 to 12 minutes. Halfway through the baking time, add Bébé's mini-cutlet to the oven.
6. Halfway through the baking time, put the peas into a saucepan, cover with water, and bring to a boil. Cook them over medium heat for 5 minutes.
7. Meanwhile, drain the sweet potatoes. Mash the potatoes and butter with a fork until you have a smooth purée.
8. Remove the turkey cutlets from the oven. Roughly chop Bébé's piece. Serve with the sweet potato purée and the peas (blended for Bébé, if necessary).

yummy tips

Roast the sweet potatoes in the oven to enhance their flavor. Cook the sweet potato cubes on the baking sheet with the turkey cutlets. To serve, mash them for Bébé and add a splash of olive oil and a sprinkle of sea salt for the grown-ups.

cod papillote with orange
papillote de cabillaud à l'orange

10   20   24ʰ   0°

Makes 2 adult portions
and 1 baby portion

2 full-size cod fillets, about 7 ounces
(200 g) each, and 1 small fillet, about ¾
ounce (20 g) for Bébé
10 cherry tomatoes
1 orange
5 fresh cilantro leaves, finely chopped
7 cups (500 g) broccoli florets

1. Preheat the oven to 350°F (180°C).
2. Place each cod fillet on a large square of aluminum foil twice its size. Make sure Bébé's piece has no bones.
3. Wash the cherry tomatoes and the orange, and cut 5 round orange slices.
4. Place 2 orange slices and 4 cherry tomatoes on each grown-up's fillet, and 1 slice and 2 cherry tomatoes on Bébé's small fillet. Squeeze the rest of the orange (discard any seeds) and coat the fish with the juice. Add the cilantro leaves to the papillotes before sealing them carefully. Bake the grown-ups' papillotes in the preheated oven for 20 minutes. Halfway through the cooking time, put Bébé's papillote into the oven.
5. Meanwhile, wash the broccoli florets. Put them into a pot with water and boil them for 10 minutes. Drain and blend them to a smooth purée.
6. Take the papillotes out of the oven. Serve the grown-up portions with the foil open. For Bébé's portion, remove the aluminum foil and serve the fish on a plate along with the broccoli purée.

yummy tips

If you want a more substantial meal, serve this dish alongside Old Fashioned Mashed Potatoes (page 68).

oven-baked salmon with fava beans, lemon and basil

saumon au four avec fèves au citron et basilic

Makes 2 adult portions and 1 baby portion

2 full-size salmon steaks, about 5 ounces (150 g) each, and 1 small steak, about ¾ ounce (20 g), for Bébé
Pinch of salt
About 2 cups (200 g) fava beans, frozen
Juice from 1 lemon
6 fresh basil leaves, chopped

1. Preheat the oven to 400°F (200°C).
2. Place each of the grown-ups' salmon steaks on a baking sheet covered with a piece of aluminum foil twice its size. Make sure Bébé's piece has no bones. Put it aside.
3. Sprinkle the grown-ups' steaks with a few grains of salt, then put them in the oven and cook for 15 minutes. Halfway through the cooking time, put the small steak for Bébé into the oven.
4. Halfway through the baking time, bring a pot of water to a boil and add the fava beans. Cook over medium heat for 7 to 10 minutes. Remove from the heat and drain. Add the lemon juice and basil.
5. Take the salmon steaks out of the oven and let cool. Serve alongside the fava beans with lemon and basil. If desired, blend to a smooth purée for Bébé.

yummy tips
This dish goes well with Carrot Purée (page 36) blended with 1 tablespoon of butter and a pinch of salt.

two-fish pie with vegetables
parmentier de deux poissons et petits légumes

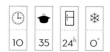

Makes 2 adult portions
and 1 baby portion

5 fingerling potatoes
⅔ cup (100 g) green beans
About 1 cup (150 g) peas, fresh or frozen
1 salmon fillet, about 7 ounces (200 g)
1 cod fillet, about 5 ounces (150 g)
6 to 7 tablespoons (100 ml) crème fraîche
2 teaspoons lemon juice
4 fresh basil leaves, chopped
1 scant tablespoon (10 g) butter
2 tablespoons milk
Pinch of salt
Pinch of ground nutmeg

1. Preheat the oven to 350°F (180° C).
2. Wash and peel the potatoes and cut them into pieces. Put the pieces into a saucepan, cover them with water, bring to a boil, and cook for 15 minutes.
3. Meanwhile, trim the green beans. Put the beans and peas into another pot, cover the vegetables with water, bring them to a boil, and cook for 3 to 4 minutes. Drain and roughly chop the vegetables with a knife.
4. Cut the fish fillets into pieces. Make sure there are no bones.
5. Place the fish pieces at the bottom of a deep ovenproof casserole. Cover with the drained green vegetables. Coat the fish and vegetables with the crème fraîche mixed with the lemon juice and basil.
6. Drain the potatoes and mash them with the butter, milk, salt, and nutmeg. Cover the casserole with the purée and bake in the middle of the preheated oven for 20 minutes.
7. If Bébé is not yet used to eating chunks of food, mash the pieces of fish.

yummy tips

Infinite combinations are possible with this recipe. Replace the cod with another firm white fish, such as monkfish or swordfish, and change up the vegetables. You might try broccoli or cauliflower, thin rounds of carrot, or even fennel, if you dare.

I can eat by myself just like a big kid!

You're finally there—at the phase every parent will know sooner or later: *Neophobia*. It's no illness, simply a tough (and natural) period when your child starts to shrink from dishes she once loved. It's also the time Bébé wants to do everything alone "like a big kid." And eating tops her list. So I created these funny little galettes (think fancy fritters) that pack in—some would say *camouflage*—some serious quantities of vegetables, an ideal situation whenever your little gourmet makes a face at a plate of her former-favorite broccoli. It's also a good way to let your little one gain some autonomy by crunching, dipping, and rolling her evening galette all by herself. After that, vegetables will once again become her favorite dish. Want to bet?

carrot-zucchini-lentil galettes
galettes de carottes-courgettes-lentilles

10 30 24ʰ 0°

Makes 20 galettes

(five servings)

For the galettes

8 carrots, about 1 pound (450 g)
About ½ cup (120 ml) orange juice
½ teaspoon ground cumin
½ cup (120 ml) vegetable stock
1½ cups (300 g) red lentils
3 zucchini, about ⅓ pound (180 g)
2 teaspoons olive oil

For the dipping sauce (1 serving)

½ cup (120 ml) plain, unsweetened
Greek yogurt
4 fresh cilantro leaves, chopped

1. Wash and peel the carrots, then cut them into rounds.
2. Put the carrots, orange juice, cumin, and vegetable stock into a saucepan and add just enough water to cover. Bring to a boil and cook for 5 minutes.
3. Add the lentils and continue to cook for 10 more minutes.
4. Meanwhile, wash the zucchini and grate them.
5. At the end of the cooking time, add the grated zucchini, drain, and blend roughly.
6. Form the mixture into small galettes, about 1¼ inches (3 cm) in diameter and ½ inch (1 cm) thick. Let them sit for a few minutes on paper towels to absorb some of their moisture.
7. Heat 1 teaspoon of the olive oil in a large nonstick pan over medium-high heat. Brown 10 galettes, cooking them 3 to 5 minutes on each side, then place them on paper towels and let them cool. Repeat.
8. Mix the yogurt with the cilantro to make a dipping sauce.
9. Serve the galettes with a small bowl of the yogurt sauce. Let Bébé eat the galettes with her fingers and dunk them into the sauce.

yummy tips

Why not make these galettes for yourself? For a light meal, serve the galettes with a grilled chicken breast dusted with cumin, paprika, and curry powder and then sprinkled with olive oil and lemon juice. Add a pinch of cayenne pepper to the yogurt sauce, and you have a flavorful dinner.

cheesy corn and carrot galettes
galettes de maïs-carottes-comté

10   30   24ʰ   0°

Makes 20 galettes
(five servings)

For the galettes
6 carrots, about 14 ounces (400 g)
½ cup (120 ml) vegetable stock
1¼ cups (200 g) corn, frozen or canned
About 1 cup (200 g) grated Comté cheese
½ teaspoon paprika
2 teaspoons olive oil

For the avocado purée
½ ripe avocado
3 drops lemon juice

1. Wash and peel the carrots, then cut them into rounds.
2. Put the carrots and vegetable stock into a saucepan and, if necessary, add water to cover. Bring to a boil, reduce the heat, and cook for 10 minutes. Add the corn kernels and cook for another 5 to 7 minutes.
3. Drain the vegetables. Add the cheese and paprika, and mix until the cheese starts to melt. Blend until you have a coarse purée.
4. Form the mixture into small galettes, about 1¼ inches (3 cm) in diameter and ½ inch (1 cm) thick. Let them sit for a few minutes on paper towels to absorb some of their moisture.
5. Heat 1 teaspoon of the olive oil in a large nonstick pan over medium-high heat. Brown 10 galettes, cooking them 3 to 5 minutes on each side, then place them on paper towels and let them cool. Repeat.
6. Just before you are ready to serve the meal, cut open the avocado and remove the pit.
7. Scoop out the avocado flesh and put it into a bowl with the lemon juice (to preserve the green color). Mash until you have a smooth purée.
8. Serve the galettes with the avocado purée. Let Bébé eat the galettes with his fingers and dunk them into the purée.

yummy tips
These galettes make a perfect starter for that special dinner with friends. If you would like them to be crisp, just leave them in the pan for an extra minute or two. Upgrade the avocado purée to a real guacamole by mixing 2 avocados with the juice of ½ lemon or lime, 2 tablespoons chopped onion, ½ teaspoon salt, and a pinch each of cumin and cayenne. Dunk without moderation.

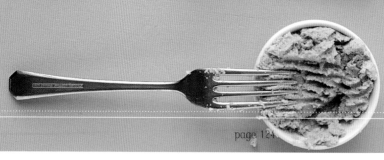

cheesy broccoli and fava bean galettes

galettes brocolis-fèves-parmesan

5   30   24ʰ   0˚

Makes 20 galettes
(five servings)

For the tomato sauce

1⅓ pounds (600 g) cherry tomatoes

1 teaspoon olive oil

½ garlic clove, finely chopped

For the galettes

6 cups (400 g) broccoli

About 2 cups (400 g) fava beans, frozen

½ cup (120 ml) vegetable stock

Just under ½ cup (100 g) grated Parmesan

4 fresh basil leaves

1 teaspoon olive oil

1. Start the sauce by washing the tomatoes and cutting them into halves.
2. In a heavy-bottomed saucepan, heat 1 teaspoon of the olive oil and add the garlic. Brown the garlic, then add the tomatoes and lower the heat. Cover and cook over medium heat for 15 to 20 minutes. Remove the pan from the heat and stir the tomatoes until you have a chunky sauce.
3. Meanwhile, for the galettes, wash the broccoli florets and cut them into small pieces.
4. Put the broccoli, fava beans, and vegetable stock into a saucepan, and add just enough water to cover. Bring to a boil, reduce the heat, and cook for 10 minutes. Drain the vegetables.
5. Mix the drained vegetables, the Parmesan, and the basil until the cheese starts to melt. Blend until you have a smooth purée (it's important to blend well because the starch in the fava beans will hold the galettes together).
6. Form the mixture into small galettes, about 1¼ inches (3 cm) in diameter and ½ inch (1 cm) thick. Let them sit for a few minutes on paper towels to absorb some of their moisture.
7. Heat the remaining 1 teaspoon olive oil over medium-high heat in a large nonstick pan. Brown 10 galettes, cooking them 3 to 5 minutes on each side, then place them on paper towels and let cool. Repeat for the remaining galettes.
8. Serve the galettes with the tomato sauce. Let Bébé eat the galettes with her fingers and dunk them in a cup of the sauce.

yummy tips

For a family lunch, serve these galettes with pan-fried chicken cutlets sprinkled with lemon and coated with tomato sauce.

"forgotten" vegetable galettes

galettes aux légumes oubliés

10 30 24ʰ 0˚

Makes 20 galettes

(five servings)

For the tomato-apple coulis

2 tomatoes, just under ½ pound (200 g)

3 to 4 sweet apples (Golden Delicious or similar), about ¾ pound (350 g)

For the galettes

1 rutabaga, just under ½ pound (200 g)

1 parsnip, about 2 ounces (60 g)

1 medium piece celery root, just under ¼ pound (100 g)

2 potatoes, just under ½ pound (200 g)

½ cup (120 ml) vegetable stock

2 teaspoons olive oil

1. Start the coulis by washing the tomatoes and apples. Peel the apples, remove the cores and any spare seeds, then cut into cubes. Cut the tomatoes into quarters.
2. Put the tomatoes and apples into a saucepan and cover them with water. Bring to a boil, cover, and simmer over low heat for 15 minutes.
3. Meanwhile, for the galettes, wash the vegetables, then peel them and cut them into pieces.
4. Put the vegetables and stock into another pan and add just enough water to cover. Bring to a boil, lower the heat, and cook for 15 minutes. Drain the vegetables. Blend until you have a chunky purée.
5. Form the mixture into small galettes, about 1¼ inches (3 cm) in diameter and ½ inch (1 cm) thick. Let them sit for a few minutes on paper towels to absorb some of their moisture.
6. Remove the tomatoes and apples from the heat and blend until you have a smooth coulis.
7. Heat 1 teaspoon of the olive oil in a large nonstick pan over medium heat. Brown 10 galettes, cooking them 3 to 5 minutes on each side, then place them on paper towels and let cool. Repeat for the remaining galettes.
8. Serve the galettes with a small side dish of tomato-apple coulis. Let Bébé eat the galettes with his fingers and dunk them into the coulis.

yummy tips

These galettes pair really well with fish—a cod fillet, a swordfish steak, a piece of monkfish—roasted in the oven with a splash of olive oil and a dash of sea salt, then topped with the tomato-apple coulis.

polenta fries with tomato and red pepper relish
bâtonnets de polenta avec tomates et poivrons rouges confits au four

Makes 7 polenta fries
(one serving) and five
3½-ounce (100 g) portions
of relish (see Yummy Tips)

**For the tomato and
red pepper relish**

*5 tomatoes or 20 cherry tomatoes, about
1⅓ pounds (600 g)*
2 red bell peppers, about ⅔ pound (300 g)
1 tablespoon olive oil

For the polenta fries

About ½ cup (120 ml) milk
*3 tablespoons and 1 teaspoon (50 g)
dried polenta*
3 to 4 tablespoons (50 g) grated Parmesan

1. Preheat the oven to 300°F (150°C).
2. Start the relish by washing the tomatoes and bell peppers. Deseed the peppers and cut them into thin slices. Cut the tomatoes into quarters. Spread the vegetables on a baking sheet covered with aluminum foil. Drizzle the vegetables with the olive oil. Roast in the middle of the oven for 30 minutes.
3. Remove the vegetables from the oven and let cool. Blend or roughly chop according to Bébé's tastes.
4. Meanwhile, bring the milk to a boil in a saucepan, stirring constantly. Remove from the heat and add the polenta and Parmesan, stirring vigorously until you have a thick, smooth purée. Pour the polenta onto a tray or plate to form a square ½ inch (1 cm) thick. Let cool, then cut into fries.
5. Serve the polenta fries with the tomato and red pepper relish. Freeze the remaining vegetables in small plastic containers.

yummy tips

I always set aside a bit of the tomato and red pepper relish to use as a chutney for grown-ups. It makes a great after-dinner treat served with a hard cheese (aged Comté or Beaufort). If apricots are in season, try adding a few to the vegetables you roast. This version pairs really well with white meat or even grilled salmon steak.

oh, pasta—kids' all-time favorite

Let's not forget pasta, the object of everyone's affection! Were you thinking that this baby food cookbook, defender of healthy eating, would pass it by? Of course not! I'm going to let you in on a secret: Pasta is chock-full of nutritious benefits and is part of a healthy diet. The thing is not to overdo it—and to know how to prepare it (you can't go wrong with a homemade tomato-basil sauce). On top of that, these quick meals are ideal for busy nights. Everyone wins!

mini-tortellini with ricotta and green vegetables
petits tortellinis, ricotta et légumes verts

5 | 10

Makes one 8-ounce (230 g) serving

¼ zucchini
¼ cup (40 g) peas, fresh or frozen
About ¼ cup (20 g) green beans,
cut into small pieces
1 teaspoon olive oil
1 teaspoon finely chopped shallots
1 teaspoon chopped fresh basil
2 tablespoons ricotta
Just under ½ cup (100 g) mini-tortellini

1. Wash the zucchini. Cut it into thin rounds, then cut the rounds into quarters.
2. In a heavy-bottomed saucepan, boil some water and toss in the zucchini, peas, and green beans. Cook for 5 to 7 minutes, then drain and set aside.
3. In the same saucepan, heat the olive oil over medium heat and add the shallots. Cook for 1 minute, then add the vegetables and continue to cook for 3 more minutes.
4. Remove the saucepan from the heat, add the basil and ricotta, reheat, and set aside.
5. Meanwhile, cook the tortellini according to the package instructions.
6. Drain the tortellini, then mix it with the vegetable and ricotta mixture. Serve the dish lukewarm on Bébé's favorite plate.

yummy tips

Want to change this up? Turn it into a baked lasagna for four instead, using fresh lasagna noodles and four times the amount of vegetables and ricotta. Take a 1-quart ovenproof casserole dish and start with a layer of lasagna noodles followed by the vegetables and ricotta, alternating layers until the dish is full. Finish with a layer of lasagna noodles, cover with a mixture of ricotta and Parmesan, and bake at 350°F (180°C) for 25 minutes.

farfalle with broccoli and parmesan
farfalles aux brocolis et au parmesan

5 | 10

Makes one 8-ounce
(230 g) serving

1½ cups (100 g) broccoli florets
1 tablespoon olive oil
1 teaspoon finely chopped shallot
2 tablespoons grated Parmesan
¼ cup (60 g) farfalle

1. Wash the broccoli florets and cut them into small pieces. Bring a pot of water to a boil and add the broccoli. Cook for 5 to 7 minutes, then drain and set aside.
2. Heat the olive oil in the same pan over medium heat and add the shallots. Cook for 1 minute, then stir in the broccoli florets and cook 3 minutes longer. Remove from the heat, add the Parmesan, reheat, and set aside.
3. Meanwhile, cook the farfalle according to the package instructions.
4. Drain the pasta, then mix it with the broccoli and Parmesan mixture.

yummy tips

This simple recipe can be prepared with almost any green vegetable. For a delicate touch, add 1 teaspoon of grated lemon zest, 1 tablespoon lemon juice, and a few fresh sage leaves per serving. Sure to impress your mother-in-law when she drops in unexpectedly for Sunday dinner!

rotelle with cherry tomatoes and mozzarella

rotelles aux tomates cerises et à la mozzarella

5 | 10

Makes one 8-ounce (230 g) serving

6 cherry tomatoes
1 tablespoon olive oil
1 teaspoon finely chopped garlic
½ cherry-size mozzarella ball, cubed
¼ cup (60 g) rotelle
3 to 4 fresh basil leaves, finely chopped

1. Wash the cherry tomatoes and cut them in half.
2. In a heavy-bottomed saucepan, heat half of the olive oil over medium heat and add the garlic. Cook for 1 minute, then add the cherry tomatoes and cook for an additional 5 minutes still over medium heat. Remove the saucepan from the heat, add the mozzarella, return the saucepan to the heat, and leave it until the mozzarella is beginning to melt.
3. Meanwhile, cook the rotelle according to the package instructions.
4. Drain the pasta, then mix with the tomato and mozzarella mixture and sprinkle with basil.

yummy tips

If Bébé's dinner is making your partner's mouth water, grill a few slices of prosciutto in the oven (5 minutes at 475°F/250°C). Tear into pieces and cover the ham with the rotelle, cherry tomatoes, and mozzarella. A real delicacy.

fusilli with summer vegetables and basil
torsades aux légumes du soleil et basilic

5 | 10

Makes one 8-ounce
(230 g) serving

3 cherry tomatoes
½ zucchini
¼ red bell pepper
1 tablespoon olive oil
1 teaspoon finely chopped garlic
3 to 4 fresh basil leaves, finely chopped
¼ cup (60 g) fusilli

1. Wash the vegetables. Cut the tomatoes in half, cut the zucchini first into rounds, then into quarters, and cut the bell pepper into small pieces.
2. In a heavy-bottomed saucepan, heat the olive oil over medium heat and add the garlic. Cook for 1 minute, add the vegetables and basil, and cook for 10 minutes more still over medium heat.
3. Meanwhile, cook the pasta according to the package instructions.
4. Drain the pasta, then mix with the vegetable sauce. If sharing with Bébé, eat while closing your eyes and dreaming of a summer evening in Provence!

yummy tips

Chop a few pitted green olives and a few slices of strong chorizo, and mix them with the vegetables. Now you have a scrumptious dinner for the grown-ups.

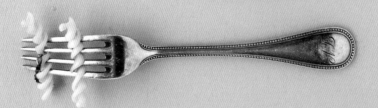

pesto penne with sugar snap peas
pennes aux pois croquants et pesto doux

5 · 10

Makes one 8-ounce (230 g) serving

1 tablespoon olive oil
¼ garlic clove
5 to 6 fresh basil leaves
1 tablespoon pine nuts
1 tablespoon grated Parmesan
⅔ cup (100 g) sugar snap peas (or snow peas) cut into small pieces
¼ cup (60 g) penne

1. Using a food processor or blender, blend the olive oil, garlic, basil, pine nuts, and Parmesan to a smooth pesto.
2. Bring a small pot of water to a boil and cook the sugar snap peas for 7 to 10 minutes.
3. Meanwhile, cook the penne according to the package instructions.
4. Drain the pasta, then mix with the peas and pesto.

yummy tips

My daughter has fun with this dish, since she's sure that penne were made especially to fit on her little fingers! For a grown-up dish, sprinkle with shavings of fresh Parmesan and toasted pine nuts.

first trip around the world

Thanks to your tasty dishes, Bébé has become a shrewd gourmet on a quest for increasingly more intense culinary pleasures. He's curious about everything, and he's more and more open to the world around him. It might be time to introduce him to the world of available flavors and help him discover foreign lands via his taste buds. At some point, it became my goal to prove that it is possible to create recipes that are inspired by foreign culinary traditions while still being perfectly suitable for little ones. I believe the development of taste should be oriented toward diversity, not limited by it. The experience of cooking these meals will prove enriching for both you and Bébé. Now boarding: a gastronomic voyage with multiple stops!

INDIA

lentil dhal with coconut milk and cilantro bulgur
dhal de lentilles rouges au lait de coco et boulgour à la coriandre

Makes five 7-ounce (200 g) servings

For the dhal
1¼ cups (250 g) red lentils
4 carrots, about ½ pound (250 g)
5 tomatoes, about 1⅓ pounds (600 g)
1 tablespoon sunflower oil
½ teaspoon finely chopped garlic
1 teaspoon turmeric
½ teaspoon ground cumin
½ teaspoon ground ginger
½ cup (120 ml) vegetable stock
1 tablespoon tomato paste
1 cup (240 ml) coconut milk

For the cilantro bulgur
About 1 cup (200 g) bulgur
1¾ cups (415 ml) water
5 fresh cilantro leaves, chopped

1. Start making the dhal by rinsing the lentils, picking them over, and discarding any stones or debris.
2. Put the lentils into a saucepan and cover them with twice their volume of water. Bring to a boil and cook for 10 minutes over medium heat. Drain and set aside.
3. Wash the carrots and tomatoes. Peel the carrots and slice into thin rounds. Finely dice the tomatoes. Set aside.
4. Start the cilantro bulgur by putting the bulgur and water into a pot. Bring to a boil, then lower the heat and cook for 10 minutes, or until the water is completely absorbed. Remove from the heat and set aside.
5. Meanwhile, in a frying pan, heat the sunflower oil over medium heat and add the garlic. Cook for 1 minute, then add the carrots and tomatoes. Sprinkle in the spices, add the vegetable stock and tomato paste, and stir well. Pour in the coconut milk, lower the heat, and simmer, uncovered, for 10 minutes.
6. Blend to a smooth purée. Add the lentils and mix well.
7. Serve the dhal with the bulgur seasoned with the cilantro.

yummy tips
Serving dhal to grown-ups? They will love it! Add just a pinch of cayenne pepper. Pairs well with grilled tandoori chicken.

MADE IN INDIA

SPAIN

vegetable paella
paella toute jaune aux legumes

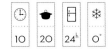

Makes five 7-ounce (200 g) servings

1 carrot, about 2 ounces (60 g)
1 red bell pepper
1 green bell pepper
⅓ cup (50 g) green beans
1 teaspoon olive oil
1 teaspoon finely chopped shallots
Pinch of saffron (or turmeric)
½ teaspoon paprika
Pinch of salt
1¼ cups (250 g) basmati rice
⅓ cup (60 g) peas, fresh or frozen
½ cup (90 g) corn, frozen or canned
1¾ cups (415 ml) water

1. Wash the vegetables. Peel and finely chop the carrot. Remove the seeds from the bell peppers and finely chop them as well. Cut the green beans into small pieces.
2. In a heavy-bottomed saucepan, heat the olive oil over medium heat and add the shallots, spices, salt, and rice. Cook for 1 to 2 minutes, until the rice is translucent.
3. Add the chopped vegetables, peas, and corn. Add the water, cover, and simmer over low heat for 15 minutes, or until the water is completely absorbed.

yummy tips

You can serve this vegetable paella with a cold yogurt sauce. Simply mix several tablespoons of plain, unsweetened Greek yogurt with a pinch of cumin and a teaspoon of ketchup. You can also easily transform this dish into traditional paella for you and your sweetie. Prepare the above recipe in a deep saucepan or wok. Add a bit of smoked paprika (depending on how spicy you like it) along with the other spices. Brown some pieces of chicken in a pan and add them to the rice when you add the water. If you are in the mood for variety, add a few jumbo shrimp or calamari and some large mussels as well. To make it really special, serve with a dry white wine such as a Spanish Pescador.

JAPAN

green vegetable and soba noodle stir-fry
sauté de legumes verts et nouilles soba

Makes five 7-ounce
(200 g) servings

*About 1 cup (150 g) each of peas,
green beans, and broccoli florets
4 Swiss chard leaves or 25 to 30 fresh
baby spinach leaves,
about 2 ounces (50 g)
½ pound soba noodles, broken into
small pieces (about 200 g)
1 tablespoon sunflower oil
½ teaspoon finely chopped garlic
1 tablespoon honey
1 tablespoon low-sodium soy sauce
1 tablespoon lemon juice*

1. Shell the peas, if using fresh. Wash the other vegetables and chop them into small pieces. Chop the chard separately.
2. Bring a pot of water to a boil and add the noodles, green beans, peas, and broccoli. Boil for 3 to 4 minutes, until the noodles are just cooked (al dente). Drain and set aside.
3. In a frying pan, heat the sunflower oil over medium heat and add the garlic. Brown the garlic 1 minute, then add the noodles and precooked vegetables. Cook for 5 minutes, stirring frequently.
4. Add the honey, soy sauce, and lemon juice as well as the Swiss chard and cook for 2 minutes more. Serve warm in Bébé's favorite bowl.

yummy tips
Add 7 ounces thinly sliced beef and a pinch of cayenne pepper to this stir-fry and you'll have a tasty and healthy supper for grown-ups!

THAILAND

mild vegetable curry with thai rice
curry tout doux de legumes et riz thaï

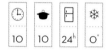

Makes five 7-ounce (200 g) servings

*1 large sweet potato,
about ⅔ pound (300 g)*
2 carrots, just under ¼ pound (100 g)
1 slice pumpkin, about ⅓ pound (180 g)
½ yellow bell pepper
1 teaspoon sunflower oil
½ teaspoon finely chopped garlic
1 cup (240 ml) coconut milk
1 teaspoon lime juice
1 teaspoon brown sugar
½ teaspoon ground ginger
4 to 5 fresh cilantro leaves
Pinch of salt
¾ cup (150 g) Thai (jasmine) rice

1. Wash the vegetables, then peel and chop them into small pieces. Bring a pot of water to a boil and add the vegetables. Cook for 5 minutes, drain, and set aside.
2. In a heavy-bottomed pot, heat the oil over medium heat and add the garlic. Brown for 1 minute and add the vegetables, coconut milk, lime juice, brown sugar, ginger, cilantro, and salt. Cover and simmer for 10 minutes.
3. Meanwhile, prepare the rice according to the package instructions.
4. Serve the vegetable curry with the rice.

yummy tips
For variety, you can use different vegetables in this recipe. Firm vegetables or root vegetables work best. A pinch of hot pepper and grated fresh ginger turns this dish into a delight for grown-ups.

Chiara, 20 months

Vera, 16 months

big-kid snacks & treats

for kids from 1 to 99

muesli crumbles

Crispy and crunchy on top, soft and gooey underneath: Beyond the health benefits of the whole grains and fresh fruit (full of vitamins, fiber, and minerals) they contain, these muesli crumbles are a veritable mine of gustatory exploration—and pleasure, too!—for little ones. These "big-kid snacks" are easy to eat: Bébé can peck at the pieces of crunchy crumble and pop the pieces of softened fruit into her mouth with her little fingers. I make them in disposable muffin tin liners; paper liners if I want to reheat them in the microwave or aluminum if they will be served cold at a picnic. For an extra treat, add a big scoop of vanilla ice cream on the side of Bébé's dish and be careful nobody tries to steal it away from her!

banana-mango muesli crumbles

muesli-crumble bananes et mangues

5   15

Makes 6 or 12 treats

6 standard (or 12 mini) muffin tin liners
2 bananas
12 slices frozen peeled mango
1¼ cups (250 g) muesli or granola with raisins
2 tablespoons butter
1 teaspoon honey

1. Preheat the oven to 425°F (210°C).
2. Line a muffin or mini-muffin tray or sheet pan with the tin liners.
3. Peel the bananas and slice them into rounds.
4. Distribute the slices of frozen mango among the muffin tin liners and add the banana slices on top.
5. Cover the fruit with the muesli and add a few small bits of butter and 1 or 2 drops of honey to each crumble.
6. Bake for 15 minutes. Make sure the crumble doesn't brown too much. You can cover the tins with aluminum foil for the final minutes, if needed.
7. Remove the crumbles from the oven and let cool. Serve warm, or once cool, put them into a freezer bag and freeze.

yummy tips
This tropical fruit crumble can be made with pineapple or lychees instead of mango.

yellow plum and chocolate muesli crumbles
muesli-crumble mirabelles et chocolat

5 | 15

Makes 6 or 12 treats

6 standard (or 12 mini) muffin tin liners
12 to 15 yellow (Mirabelle) plums,
about 2 ½ pounds (1 kg)
1 tablespoon sugar
1 ¼ cups (250 g) crunchy chocolate chip
muesli
2 tablespoons butter
1 teaspoon honey

1. Preheat the oven to 425°F (210°C).
2. Place the muffin tin liners in muffin tins or on a sheet pan.
3. Wash and pit the plums, then cut them into quarters.
4. Distribute the plums among the muffin liners and sprinkle with sugar.
5. Cover the fruit with the crunchy chocolate chip muesli and add a few small bits of butter and 1 to 2 drops of honey to each crumble.
6. Bake for 15 minutes. Make sure the crumble doesn't brown too much. You can cover the tins with aluminum foil for the final minutes, if needed.
7. Remove the crumbles from the oven and let cool. Serve warm, or once cool, put them into a freezer bag and freeze.

yummy tips

Can't find crunchy chocolate chip muesli? If you don't want to miss out on the chocolate, simply chop a few squares of your favorite chocolate and add it to the muesli.

raspberry-mint muesli crumbles
muesli-crumble framboises et menthe

5 15

Makes 6 or 12 treats

6 standard (or 12 mini) muffin tin liners
1 pound (450 g) raspberries
1 tablespoon sugar
6 fresh mint leaves
1¼ cups (250 g) crunchy muesli with
dried fruit
2 tablespoons butter
1 teaspoon honey

1. Preheat the oven to 425°F (210°C).
2. Line a muffin or mini-muffin tray or sheet pan with the tin liners.
3. Wash the raspberries well and distribute among the muffin liners. Sprinkle with sugar. Finely mince the mint leaves and sprinkle them over the raspberries.
4. Cover the fruit with crunchy muesli and add a few small bits of butter and 1 or 2 drops of honey to each.
5. Bake for 15 minutes. Make sure the crumble doesn't brown too much. You can cover the tins with aluminum foil for the final minutes, if needed.
6. Remove the crumbles from the oven and let cool. Serve warm, or once cool, put them into a freezer bag and freeze.

yummy tips

You can also make this recipe with strawberries or blueberries when they're in season. For a quick dessert (no cooking required), fill small glasses with a layer of fruit, then fromage blanc or plain, unsweetened Greek yogurt, a couple drops of honey, and crunchy muesli on top. Quick, attractive, and above all, delicious!

melon-peach kabobs
brochettes melon-pêche

Makes 2 treats

5

2 slices melon
1 yellow peach
2 wooden skewers

1. Peel and deseed the melon, then cut it into small cubes.
2. Wash the peach and remove the pit, then cut it into small pieces.
3. Slide the fruit onto wooden skewers, alternating melon cubes and peach pieces.
4. Before serving the kabobs to Bébé, use scissors to cut off the sharp tip of the skewers.

strawberry-raspberry kabobs
brochettes fraise-framboise

Makes 2 treats

5

5 strawberries
10 large raspberries
2 wooden skewers

1. Wash the strawberries well, remove any leaves, and cut them in half.
2. Wash the raspberries well, inside and out.
3. Slide the berries onto wooden skewers, alternating strawberries and raspberries.
4. Before serving the kabobs to Bébé, use scissors to cut off the sharp tip of the skewers.

mango-banana kabobs
brochettes mangue-banane

Makes 2 treats

5

½ mango
1 banana
2 wooden skewers

1. Without breaking through the peel, score the flesh of the half mango first lengthwise and then widthwise. Invert the mango half by pressing the peel side, then slide the knife along the peel to remove the mango cubes that are now sticking up.
2. Peel the banana and slice it into rounds.
3. Slide the fruit onto wooden skewers, alternating cubes and rounds. Before serving the kabobs to Bébé, use scissors to cut off the sharp tip of the skewers.

clementine-grape kabobs
brochettes raisin-clémentine

Makes 2 treats

5

10 seedless green grapes
1 clementine
2 wooden skewers

1. Wash the grapes and cut them in half.
2. Peel the clementine and remove as many of the white filaments as possible. Separate the sections.
3. Slide the fruit onto wooden skewers, alternating grapes and sections of clementine. Before serving the kabobs to Bébé, use scissors to cut off the sharp tip of the skewers.

lemon-yogurt cake

gateau au citron et au yaourt

10   45

Serves 8 to 10

½ cup (120 ml) plain,
unsweetened Greek yogurt
1 cup (200 g) sugar
1 vanilla bean
2 eggs
3 ½ tablespoons melted butter
Pinch of salt
1 ¼ cups (250 g) all-purpose flour
Juice from 1 lemon

1. Preheat the oven to 350°F (180°C).
2. Mix the yogurt and sugar in a bowl.
3. With a knife, open the vanilla bean lengthwise and scrape out the seeds into the bowl.
4. Break the eggs into the yogurt mixture and beat them in vigorously.
5. Add the butter and salt, and mix. Then add the flour in small amounts, stirring each time until the batter is smooth. Stir in the lemon juice.
6. Pour the cake batter into an 10-inch (25 cm) silicone mold or buttered cake pan. Bake for 45 minutes.
7. Verify that the cake is cooked by inserting a toothpick or knife into its center: If the toothpick comes out clean, the cake is ready.
8. Let it sit for a few minutes before removing it from cake pan.
9. Serve the cake warm with a fruit kabob!

yummy tips

Try variants of this cake by replacing the lemon juice with 3 tablespoons of cocoa powder, the juice of ½ orange, or ½ cup frozen raspberries.

Maya's mini-muffins
les mini-muffins de Maya

| 10 | 15 |

Makes 20 mini-muffins

20 mini-muffin tin liners
4 eggs
1 ¼ cups (250 g) sugar
1 vanilla bean
6 tablespoons water
2 teaspoons and a pinch of baking soda
1 ¼ cups (250 g) flour

1. Preheat the oven to 350°F (180°C).
2. Place the muffin tin liners in muffin tins or on a sheet pan.
3. Break the eggs into a bowl and add the sugar. Beat vigorously.
4. With a knife, open the vanilla bean lengthwise and scrape out the seeds into the bowl.
5. Add the water and continue to beat the mixture. Add the baking soda, then incorporate the flour gradually, mixing constantly.
6. Fill the muffin tin liners halfway with batter. Bake for 15 minutes.
7. Verify that the mini-muffins are done by sticking a toothpick or a knife into their center. If the toothpick comes out clean, the muffins are ready.
8. Remove the muffins from oven and let them cool on a rack before you serve them with fruit kabobs.

yummy tips

You can turn these kids' mini-muffins into light *financiers* by adding 3 tablespoons and 1 teaspoon (50 g) almond powder in with the flour. Very, very enjoyable, but only recommended for babies older than twelve months and with no family history of food allergy.

oatmeal cookies
cookies aux flocons d'avoine

10   10

Makes 16 to 20 cookies

1 stick (110 g) butter
1¼ cups (250 g) oats
⅔ cup (150 g) brown sugar
⅔ cup (100 g) raisins
¾ cup (150 g) flour
5 tablespoons water

1. Preheat the oven to 350°F (180°C).
2. Melt the butter.
3. Put the oats into a mixing bowl, then pour the melted butter over them and stir.
4. Add the sugar and raisins, then incorporate the flour gradually. Mix in the water. Your batter should be firm.
5. Make small balls of cookie mixture and place them 2 inches apart on a baking sheet lined with parchment paper. Flatten them slightly and bake in the center of the oven for 10 minutes.
6. Remove the cookies from the oven and let them cool on a rack before serving with fruit kabobs.

yummy tips

Feeling naughty? Replace the raisins with chocolate chips . . . Shhh! We won't tell Dr. Lalau Keraly!

milkshakes: the basics . . .

milk-shake–la base . . .

Makes two 5-ounce
(150 ml) servings

½ cup (120 ml) plain, unsweetened
Greek yogurt
½ cup (120 ml) milk

strawberries and a pinch of brown sugar

6 to 8 strawberries, washed well and leaves removed

1 teaspoon brown sugar

mango and banana

½ mango, skinned and pitted

½ banana with skin removed

blueberries and raspberries

2 tablespoons blueberries, washed well

10 raspberries, washed well

peach and a drop of honey

1 peach, pitted and skinned

1 teaspoon honey

1. Put the yogurt, milk, and fruit into a bowl, as well as any sugar or honey (if you're serving to children twelve months and up).
2. Blend well until there are no lumps.
3. If the milkshake is too thick, add a bit more milk and stir.

toasted fruit pockets

Because there is nothing more satisfying than a child taking immense pleasure from a meal, I came up with these "fruit pockets," which elicited a hip-hip-hooray from my children and their friends. The most fabulous thing about these fruity snacks is, of course, that they are fun. Obviously, these pockets are full of the nutritional benefits of fresh fruit, which helps your child fill up on vitamins, minerals, and fiber. But at this exploratory stage when Bébé begins to enjoy seeing familiar objects appear and reappear, watching her plate become a hide-and-seek playground will be an unmatchable pleasure for her. And if she manages to hold these little fruit pockets in her own little foodie hands, the bonus is another step toward independence. Everything about these snacks is good!

basic recipe

recette de base

Makes 1 fruit pocket

2 slices whole wheat or whole grain bread
½ teaspoon butter
One of the fruit fillings
on the following pages

1. Butter the slices of bread on one side.
2. Spread the fruit filling (see recipes on the following pages) on the buttered side of one of the slices and cover with the other slice, buttered side toward the fruit.
3. Place the fruit pocket in a sandwich press, close, and let cook for about 3 minutes.
4. Remove the fruit pocket from the grill and let cool before cutting diagonally in half.
5. Bébé can eat these fruit pockets all on her own, at home, at a picnic, on the road . . . it's the most practical snack ever!

yummy tips

When you bring your favorite toasted fruit pockets on a picnic with you, let them cool entirely before wrapping them in aluminum foil. And don't cut them in half, or the fruit will ooze out before snack time! These will keep for a couple of hours in a plastic bag.

apple-banana filling
garniture pomme-banane

½ apple
½ banana

5   3

24ʰ   0°

1. Wash the apple and remove the core and any spare seeds. Grate the apple and squeeze the pulp between your hands to remove some of the juice, which would otherwise make the fruit pocket soggy.
2. Peel the banana and slice it into rounds.
3. Place the grated apple and the banana slices on a slice of buttered bread, cover with the other slice, and cook according to the basic recipe.

mango-lychee filling
garniture mangue-litchi

4 slices mango
3 lychees, peeled and pitted

5   3

24ʰ   0°

1. Cut the pitted lychees into quarters and place them on a paper towel for a few minutes to absorb some of their juice. Wet fruit will result in a soggy fruit pocket.
2. Place the slices of mango and the lychees on a slice of buttered bread, cover with the other slice, and cook according to the basic recipe.

vanilla-pear filling
garniture poire-vanille

½ pear
1 vanilla bean

5 · 3

24ʰ · 0°

1. Wash the pear and remove the core and any spare seeds. Store one half of the pear in plastic wrap in the refrigerator. Slice the other half into thin slices.
2. With a knife, open the vanilla bean lengthwise and scrape out the seeds.
3. Place the pear slices and the vanilla bean seeds on a slice of buttered bread, cover with the other slice of bread, and cook according to the basic recipe.

fig and honey filling
garniture figue au miel

1 very ripe fig
1 teaspoon honey

5 · 3

24ʰ · 0°

1. Cut the fig in half and scrape out all of the red pulp. Discard the skin.
2. Spread the fig pulp on a slice of buttered bread, add the honey, cover with the other slice of bread, and cook according to the basic recipe.

first birthday

Pfffffftttt! In a spray of spittle, Bébé is already blowing out her first candle. Along with her first teeth, her first words, and her first steps, this is a marvelous moment. And just because she's only twelve months old doesn't mean she has to stick to her usual apple-banana compote! At one year, you can serve her a real big-kid birthday treat. Because, once in a while, it's great to indulge in something exceptional—and to do so as a family. So here is my favorite selection of *crème de la crème* birthday cakes for "big bébé gourmets"! They have brought joy to my daughter's and son's, my nieces' and nephews' birthday parties . . . and to their respective parents. Get ready for sticky faces and hands!

my grandmother's birthday cake
gateau d'anniversaire de ma grand-mère

Serves 8 to 10

For the sponge cake
4 eggs
1¼ cups (250 g) sugar
1 vanilla bean
6 tablespoons water
2 teaspoons and a pinch of baking soda
1¼ cups (250 g) flour

For the icing
2 vanilla beans
13.5 fluid ounces (400 ml) heavy cream
1 teaspoon vanilla extract
1½ teaspoons sugar
6 tablespoons raspberry or strawberry jam
1 pound (450 g) raspberries, washed well
And one magnificent birthday candle!

1. Preheat the oven to 350°F (180°C).
2. Break the eggs into a bowl and add the sugar. With a knife, open the vanilla bean lengthwise and scrape out the seeds into the bowl. Beat well. Add the water and continue to beat the mixture. Add the baking soda, and incorporate the flour gradually.
3. Pour the batter into a buttered 10-inch (25 cm) round cake pan. Bake in the preheated oven for 45 minutes. Verify that the sponge cake is cooked through by inserting a toothpick or knife into the center: If the toothpick comes out clean, the cake is done. Let the cake cool in the pan, then transfer it to a cooling rack.
4. Next, prepare the icing. With a knife, open the vanilla beans lengthwise and scrape out the seeds.
5. Put the cream, vanilla extract, sugar, and vanilla bean seeds into a bowl. Whip this mixture until it becomes firm whipped cream. (I advise using an electric mixer.) Let it sit in the refrigerator for 30 minutes.
6. When the sponge cake has cooled completely, cut it horizontally into 3 discs, each about ½" thick.
7. Take the top disc, always a little rounded, turn it over, and place it on a serving dish or large plate. Spread 2 tablespoons of jam on top (cut side), add a layer of vanilla whipped cream, then half of the fresh raspberries. Place the second sponge cake disc on top and repeat the previous step, reserving 9 raspberries for the top. Finish with the last sponge cake disc.
8. Cover the cake entirely with the remaining whipped cream and decorate with the reserved fresh raspberries and the birthday candle. Let sit 1 hour before serving.

chocolate-covered dried fruit treats

bonbons de fruits secs en robe de chocolat

15   5

Makes 20 treats

20 mini-muffin tin liners
10 dried apricots
⅓ cup (60 g) raisins
4 prunes
3½ ounces (100 g) milk chocolate

1. Place the tin liners on a tray.
2. Chop the dried fruit.
3. Place the chocolate in a metal bowl or small pan and place in a pot full of water to create a double boiler. Bring the water to a boil and allow the chocolate to melt, stirring gently from time to time (no water should spill into the chocolate).
4. Once the chocolate is melted, add the dried fruit. Mix well, until all the fruit is covered with chocolate.
5. Using 2 teaspoons, drop a small amount of chocolate-covered fruit into each tin liner.
6. Place the tray immediately into the refrigerator and let the treats chill 2 hours before serving.

yummy tips

These treats are so easy to make. I frequently make an adult version by adding chopped hazelnuts and using dark chocolate. They're perfect with coffee after a nice meal, and much more nutritious than an ordinary chocolate truffle.

caramel-covered fresh fruit lollipops
sucettes de fruits frais au caramel

10   5

Makes 20 lollipops

20 wooden skewers
20 strawberries
3 sweet-tart apples
(Royal Gala, Pink Lady)
1¼ cups (250 g) sugar
⅔ cup (160 ml) water

1. Use scissors to cut off the sharp ends of the skewers and cover a dish with wax paper.
2. Wash the strawberries and remove any leaves. Wash the apples, remove the cores and any spare seeds, and cut into small cubes. Slide a strawberry and two apple cubes onto a wooden skewer.
3. Now get any children out of the kitchen. You are going to make caramel and it's very, very hot! Pour the sugar and water into a pot. Bring to a boil without stirring. When the sugar begins to brown, stir delicately. As soon as the caramel is golden in color, remove the pot from the heat and set it in cold water to stop the caramelization.
4. Caramel solidifies rapidly, so don't waste any time: Dip your fresh fruit lollipops one by one into the caramel. Lay them on the dish covered in wax paper to cool and harden.
5. Once cool, arrange the lollipops in a vase or a sturdy glass and let the children help themselves to these crunchy, fruity lollipops.

yummy tips
You can make these lollipops using any firm and slightly tart fruit. Forget about bananas, but melon, nectarines, and apricots work well.

raspberry roll
roulé aux framboises

10   8

Serves 10

3 eggs
1 cup (200 g) sugar
2 teaspoons and a pinch of baking soda
¾ cup (200 g) flour
¼ cup (60 ml) milk
1 pound (450 g) raspberries, washed
well and crushed

1. Preheat the oven to 400°F (200°C) and line a jelly roll pan or rectangular 10½ x 15½-inch (30 x 40 cm) oven-safe dish with parchment paper.
2. Break the eggs into a bowl and add the sugar. Beat with an electric mixer until light and airy.
3. Stirring constantly, add the baking soda and flour. Pour in the milk and whip lightly until the batter is smooth.
4. Pour the batter into the pan. Bake in the preheated oven for 8 to 10 minutes. It should be springy to the touch and beginning to shrink away from the sides of the pan.
5. Remove the sponge cake from the oven and turn it out onto wax paper on your countertop. Spread the crushed raspberries evenly over the surface and, starting with the short side, roll the cake until you have a formed a jelly roll.
6. Place the roll in the refrigerator with the seam underneath. Let it sit for 1 hour.
7. Cut the roll into ¾-inch (2 cm) slices and serve!

yummy tips

No fresh fruit in the refrigerator? In lieu of raspberries, you can fill your roll with any thick compote, such as those on pages 24—35.

f.a.q. with dr. jean lalau keraly
& nutritional information

F.A.Q. with Dr. Jean Lalau Keraly

fruit

I usually peel all fruit. Is this best for my baby?

Let's not forget that the vitamins and minerals in fruit are found in high concentrations in and under the peel. By removing the skin and outer layer of pulp with a knife, 25 percent of the benefits of these nutrients are lost. I recommend using only organic fruit or fruit that has not been treated after harvest, because pesticides stay on the peel. Always thoroughly wash fruit before eating it. And if the outermost layer is decidedly unappealing to you, scrape it off lightly with a sharp knife in order to preserve as much of the fruit's nutritional value as possible.

Some compotes are raw. Can my baby eat them?

When your baby first begins to eat solid foods, raw fruit should be avoided because it is more difficult to digest than cooked fruit. However, once the change in your baby's diet is underway (around five to six months) she can indulge in ripe, raw fruit, which abounds with nutritional and sensorial benefits. What a giant step it is, in learning the pleasures of eating, for your baby to grip juicy slices of peach or melon to taste, suckle, and munch at will.

Fruit before bed—is that such a good idea?

You must be thinking of the recommendation to avoid giving children sugary foods in the evening because sugar (glucose) is a stimulant incompatible with bedtime. However, the sugar in fruit (fructose) is different from processed sugar and doesn't have the same disadvantages as the glucose found in sweets. On the contrary, it even stimulates digestion—perfect for a good night's sleep!

Should I sweeten my baby's yogurt with honey rather than white sugar?

Once your baby is one year old, yes! Not only does it take less honey than white sugar to sweeten a serving of yogurt, honey is sweeter than white sugar and has fewer calories per teaspoon. Honey also has well-known antibacterial and immunity-boosting qualities, ideal for helping little bodies protect themselves against illness, especially in the winter.

If I mix fresh fruit and dairy, won't it be difficult for my baby to digest?

You must be referring to the notion that dairy and raw fruit can both be difficult to digest, and therefore the idea of giving Baby the two combined feels risky. No worries: You can use formula specially adapted to your child's needs. From six months on, blended raw fruit is perfectly suitable for babies.

Can apricot compote give my baby a bellyache?

Apricots are slightly acidic, but if they are nice and ripe, there is no reason to worry for your little one. In fact, apricots are among the first fruits introduced to an infant's diet because they are easy on the tummy. The acidity of the apricot actually stimulates gastric secretions, facilitating digestion. And apricot fibers are soft and well tolerated by the fragile intestines of an infant.

What is the nutritional value of dried apricots for my baby?

Dried apricots—like all dried fruit—are rich in fiber, trace elements, and fatty acids. They contain five times more carbohydrates than fresh apricots, which make them an ideal snack when you need an energy boost. They are also rich in beta-carotene, potassium, and iron, and have antioxidant and antianemic qualities.

Are tropical fruits allergenic?

Long live tropical fruit! Contrary to what was commonly believed for many years, recent studies show that tropical fruits are no more likely than other fruits to cause food allergies. And they have the advantage of being available in winter when other fruits are out of season. Aside from their rich vitamin content, they go well in sweet-and-savory dishes, which is ideal for introducing little ones to new recipes.

Isn't banana-mango compote a little exotic for an infant?

Exotic, perhaps, but from whose point of view? For an Ecuadorian infant, an apple-pear compote would be exotic. Mangoes and bananas are excellent first fruits to introduce, and they're no more allergenic than common fruit. Pineapple, however, should probably come later, not because it is allergenic but because of its fibrous texture.

I'm allergic to raspberries. Should I avoid giving them to my baby as well?

We often confuse food allergies with food intolerances. Very few people have a real food allergy, which in the 30 minutes following ingestion brings on a violent allergic reaction such as swelling, vomiting, or difficulty breathing. It is possible to have an intolerance for a certain food at one point in time, without ever having a problem after that. The opposite is also true. Raspberries are histamine-liberators. We all have histamines in our body. Certain foods, alone or combined with other foods in a meal, can induce a peak release of histamines that can cause a rash, for example. However, this is not the same as a real food allergy, for you or for your baby! Simply introduce this food slowly. If all goes well, there's no need to deprive your baby.

Can blueberries be allergenic?

Blueberries, as their name implies, are berries, and thus subject to berries' reputation of being allergenic. However, many studies have found that unless your child has a history of allergies, berries are no more allergenic for infants than other common fruits. You can therefore give your baby blueberries without fear. Just make sure you introduce them into the diet gradually in small amounts.

vegetables

Shouldn't I always peel the vegetables I feed to my baby?

You certainly can peel the vegetables you feed to your baby, but keep this in mind: Just as with fruit, most of the vitamins contained in vegetables are concentrated in their peel and just underneath. It would be a shame to forgo so many of the nutritional benefits of your vegetables by removing their thick outer layer. If your baby doesn't like the skin, you can either blend your purée more finely or lightly scrape the vegetables with a sharp knife to remove just a thin layer, preserving as many vitamins as possible.

Isn't it best to steam vegetables?

Better yet, cook your vegetables in a pot with a small amount of water at the bottom. Not only is this technique quicker than steaming or boiling, but the water left over from cooking can be incorporated into the purée. Why would you want to do that? Because during cooking some of the vitamins dissolve into the water. By using the water to mix the purée, you enrich the already nutritious purée further. Your baby will feast on a vegetable dish full of vitamins, minerals, and trace elements.

I've heard that certain vegetables contain nitrates. Is this true?

Yes and no. Vegetables with high nitrate content include leafy greens such as spinach and endive. Tomatoes, mushrooms, and peas are low in nitrates, while green beans are somewhere in between. As much as possible, use organic or market fresh vegetables (which are often less rich in nitrates) for your purées. That said, let's clarify. Nitrates themselves pose no health risk. It's nitrites (modified nitrates) that do. It is nearly impossible to be contaminated by vegetables treated with nitrates. However, the danger lies in the vegetable purée that has been sitting in the fridge for more than 24 hours and whose nitrates have had time to transform into nitrites. For infants younger than twelve months, vegetable dishes must be eaten right away or frozen as soon as they are cooled.

There are always lots of potatoes in jars of commercial baby food. Will my baby really like "pure" purées?

You bring up an interesting point here: the systematic addition of potatoes to most store-bought baby food. While potatoes are wonderful with a touch of butter, don't forget that they are not vegetables but starch, and as such, less rich in vitamins but much richer in carbohydrates. I might add that their neutral flavor does nothing to develop the flavor palette of your child. If manufacturers use large amounts of potato in their recipes, it's in part to dull the taste of some flavorful vegetables, thus contributing to the homogenization of food in our culture, but more important, it's because potatoes are cheaper than "real" vegetables. Therefore, on the contrary, serving your baby "pure" purée has nutritional benefits and encourages the discovery of new flavors.

What's all this about parsnips?

Indeed, few people are familiar with this "forgotten" vegetable, whose heyday was from antiquity through the Middle Ages. A member of the carrot family, the parsnip was a staple food source, especially in northeastern Europe. The parsnip is still popular in those regions, thanks to its nutritional value. Unlike carrots, parsnips are rich in fiber and help fight constipation. And they cook much faster than carrots, which is helpful when Baby is howling for the next meal!

Why should I use sweet potatoes instead of potatoes? Aren't they allergenic?

Sweet potatoes, or yams, are comparatively low in calories, have a higher nutrient content than white potatoes, and are just as easy to prepare. And their slightly sweet flavor is pleasant and comforting for little mouths. Sweet potatoes are a tuber and have little allergic potential for infants.

"Forgotten" vegetables—sure, why not? But what's wrong with good old-fashioned mashed potatoes?

While potatoes shouldn't be eliminated entirely from the infant diet, remember that they have much less nutritional value than other vegetables. Our culture today favors starchy foods such as rice, potatoes, bread, and pasta. Our role—and yours, as a parent—is to help your baby learn to eat "real" vegetables, in purées and then in whole pieces. Not to mention that rutabagas and celery root are much more flavorful than the rather neutral-tasting potato.

We don't often serve pumpkin to babies. Should I serve it to my baby?

Pumpkin is not only rich nutritionally speaking, it also has a lovely nutty flavor. It is a great source of vitamins A, C, D, and E, as well as trace elements such as phosphorus, magnesium, potassium, and iron. In addition, pumpkin contains unsaturated fatty acids and good amounts of carotene (twice as much as in carrots), which is excellent for your baby's skin.

Can peas give my baby a bellyache?

Yes and no. When solid foods are first introduced, a baby's digestive tract is not yet mature enough to handle fibrous or gas-producing vegetables such as peas or cabbage. But it's just a matter of time. Once your baby is well accustomed to solid foods (at six to seven months old), peas will no longer be difficult to digest.

Will cauliflower make my baby colicky?

It's not the cauliflower itself but the sulfur—a trace element with detoxifying and antibacterial properties—it contains that makes this delicious vegetable sometimes difficult to digest. To ward off bloating, change the water in your pot partway through cooking (much of the sulfur will go out with the first round of water), and add a few grains of cumin or fennel to your mixture. These spices help combat gas.

I've heard that bell peppers aren't good for babies. Is this true?

Bell peppers are, indeed, difficult to digest when eaten raw and unpeeled, hence the rumor that they are not a good food for infants. However, once peppers are cooked, peeled, and seeded, they are perfectly suitable for all. Considering how beneficial bell peppers can be, it would be a shame to leave them out of your baby's diet. However, it's a good idea to wait to add them until solid foods have been well integrated. When your baby is eight to nine months old you can start to work the peppers in.

Do tomatoes have better nutritional value raw or cooked?

Either cooked or raw, tomatoes are full of nutritional benefits, thanks to high doses of vitamin C (found in the viscous casing of their seeds), vitamin E, potassium, and folic acid, and they are low in calories. However, it is true that cooked tomatoes—including sauces and concentrates—are richer than raw tomatoes in the carotenoid lycopene, a powerful antioxidant.

Won't fava beans give my baby gas?

Fava beans are indeed very rich in fiber, which activates the bowel and facilitates movement through the intestine. This increased activity can sometimes irritate an infant's fragile intestine. Keep in mind that most of the fiber in the beans is contained in their outermost casings. Thus, to eliminate much of the fiber, you can simply remove the first casing of the bean or purchase frozen fava beans without the casing.

Favism (G6PD deficiency), an extremely rare disease, is said to be linked to fava beans. Why risk feeding them to my baby?
Fava beans are not the cause of this hereditary disease, but their consumption can sometimes spark symptoms (destruction of red blood cells) in carriers of a certain chromosomal mutation. This disease is mainly found in families of Mediterranean origin. If this disease has occurred within your family, ask your family doctor for advice.

Is corn suitable for babies?
Not only is corn full of nutrients, the unprocessed version is gluten-free. This is good news for children with allergies, as well as for all infants, who should not be exposed to gluten before six months of age. Corn is thus a strong candidate for the top ten superstar foods for babies!

Shouldn't I be worried about genetically modified corn?
Indeed, we should be careful about what foods we eat and those we feed to our children. Check the label on the corn products you buy (fresh, frozen, canned, syrup) and make sure that it says "No GMOs." Better yet, buy only organic corn products.

Can I serve my baby store-bought ratatouille and other dishes if I don't have time to cook?
Beware of dishes you don't make yourself, as they can contain large amounts of extra salt and fat. While these ingredients make dishes more appetizing for adults, they are unsuitable in large quantities for your baby.

In addition, such dishes tend to contain artificial coloring and preservatives, which are not generally found in baby food. If you are really short on time, read the list of ingredients carefully and try to choose dishes with as few additives (including salt and fat) as possible.

I've never heard of red lentils before. Why should I serve them to my baby?
The differences among varieties of lentils are subtle. All lentils are rich in proteins and fiber. Red lentils, in addition to their lovely color, are tender and thus have a shorter cooking time than their green cousins. That's a clear advantage when every minute counts.

meat
Isn't pork just a fatty meat?
Away with misconceptions! Pork is no fattier than other meats. On average, a portion of pork has about the same number of calories as a portion of chicken, which is reputed to be lean meat. In addition, most of the fat found in pork is composed of unsaturated fatty acids, which are helpful in preventing cardiovascular disease. Finally, pork is a good source of high-quality proteins. An average portion of pork covers half of an adult's daily protein needs. Beware, however, of sausage, bacon, ribs, and other pork products that are indeed high in salt and fat.

Will my baby like the taste of lamb? I personally find the taste too strong.
Taste and color are linked to personal preference. But just because you don't like lamb doesn't mean your child won't. Give him a chance to try it, for the sake of the nutritional benefits lamb has to offer. A side

of Carrot and Cumin Purée (page 67) might be a nice addition. And keep in mind that all tastes are acquired. You may not think you like lamb, but you might be surprised to find you enjoy the recipes in this book.

fish and shellfish

Is it absolutely necessary for my baby to eat fish?

That depends on her age. From six to seven months on, your baby will need sources of protein other than milk. Fish is very good in this role. It is full of omega-3, which plays a crucial role in sight and brain development. Indeed, a child's brain continues to grow until it reaches the size of an adult brain, around five years of age. It is easy to see that eating fish can be extremely beneficial for your little one.

Isn't the flavor of salmon too strong for an infant?

Why be afraid of introducing your baby to strong flavors? The wider the range of tastes your baby gets accustomed to, the better he will be prepared to enjoy the diversity of food later on. If your baby doesn't like the taste of salmon the first time, don't be discouraged. Try it again at a later date.

I boycott tuna for environmental reasons. What can I replace it with? Is my baby missing out on a super food?

It's true, nutritional value among the different kinds of fish varies some, but there are nonetheless important similarities. It's fish itself that is a super food, with a miraculously low lipid content (plenty of omega-3) and a protein content equal to that of meat—not to mention the phosphorus, magnesium, and

iodine fish contains. You can therefore easily replace tuna with cod or salmon, for example.

When can my baby start eating shrimp?

In general, the addition of crustaceans such as shrimp to your baby's diet is not advised before twelve months of age, and families with a history of food allergies may want to check with their pediatrician. Indeed, crustaceans can provoke severe allergic reactions—as can peanuts and kiwis—such as eczema or anaphylactic shock. If all other solid foods have been well tolerated by your child, there is no reason why you shouldn't add shrimp at twelve months. However, it is a good idea to give very small quantities at first so that you can observe your child's reaction in the minutes, hours, and days that follow. If all goes well, you can serve Jenny's Vegetable Paella (page 138) with shrimp!

starches

What is bulgur?

Originally found in the Balkan region, bulgur is made of parboiled wheat that is then dried, hulled, and more or less finely crushed. Bulgur is a good source of vitamin B, which helps strengthen the immune system. This starch also contains minerals such as iron, which helps stave off illness. Finally, it's easy to digest and quick to prepare, a useful advantage when you're in a hurry to feed Baby.

What are soba noodles? Are they good for my baby?

Soba noodles are made from wheat and buckwheat flour. While its name can be misleading, buckwheat is not actually a variety of wheat. Gluten-free and easy to digest, buckwheat is suitable for people with an intolerance to gluten or who are subject to colic. Furthermore, a Canadian study has shown a favorable effect of buckwheat on blood sugar levels, which is good news for diabetics. Not to mention that buckwheat is a good source of minerals, such as fortifying phosphorus. Finally, in Japanese culture, soba noodles are eaten on the New Year to ensure a long life.

Won't so much rice in the evening before bed constipate my child?

In children who frequently eat rice, the constipation culprit is the lack of natural fibers found in vegetables and fruits, not the rice. Rice is an excellent starch that's rich in minerals and vitamin B5. A dish of rice and stewed mixed vegetables is a nutritious meal that is ideal for your child's digestive system. If you are still worried about constipation, choose whole-grain rice, which is rich in fiber and will help prevent bowel sluggishness.

cheese

Isn't ricotta one of the cheeses that harbors dangerous bacteria?

You are probably thinking of listeria, a bacteria that can develop in raw-milk cheeses, dried meats and sausages, and foods for which the cold chain can be compromised between manufacturer and retail store. Listeria can indeed cause serious infections in very young infants. However, it can't survive high temperatures, so you can, for example, add ricotta to a dish when you are cooking it. That way, you'll have food safety and sensory pleasure guaranteed!

Isn't Parmesan too salty for my baby?

You are right: Salt should not be added to your little one's diet, not until at least two years

of age. But the goal is not to eliminate all natural sources of salt, which is beneficial for your child. A baby is simply not able to eliminate a lot of excess salt, which is why the salt naturally found in vegetables and other foods is sufficient for her. This is why pediatricians say, and repeat, that you should not add salt to your infant's food. The salt in Parmesan will naturally season the dish, so you don't have to add any more than that.

sweets

Am I encouraging a junk-food diet if I give my child cookies?

It's true, we hear a lot about the overconsumption of sugary (and greasy) foods, especially in children, and the facts are there. But try to remain levelheaded and keep from giving in to paranoia. A little cookie from time to time never made a child obese. Especially not a homemade cookie. You can control its ingredients (no additives or hidden starch) and how much sugar and fat go into it. The less processed food (rich in hidden sugars, fats, and salt) your child eats, the better prepared he will be as an adult to maintain a balanced diet.

Shouldn't I think twice before giving my baby candy?

There's candy, and there's *candy*. If we're talking industrial candy that's full of processed sugar, indeed you should keep your children as far away as possible from these "foods" that provide them with nothing but cavities. In this book, we include good candy, little treats to make your baby happy or to make it a special day. But they are healthy, too. Raisins and chocolate are filled with good things. And you can even choose the chocolate you buy according to its sugar content: dark, milk, white . . . The natural candy in this book is soft and easy to eat. So you can give your baby a piece to taste and know that it's safe.

spices

Isn't there a chance my baby could be allergic to cinnamon or cumin?

Don't worry: Cinnamon and cumin (and mild spices in general) pose no health risk for infants—on the contrary! Cinnamon is rich in antioxidants and fiber. In addition, it stimulates your baby's taste buds and offers an opportunity to learn a new flavor. I would advise sticking to real Ceylon cinnamon, which comes from Sri Lanka (it's ochre yellow and crumbly), if you can find it. Chinese cinnamon (the hard, dark brown sticks) is less sweet, more bitter, and often less nutrient rich. Cumin offers your baby a new flavor, as well as a soothing natural remedy for tummy aches.

Is it true that vanilla will help my baby sleep?

Indeed, aside from its pleasant sweet flavor, vanilla has sedative qualities. It can be used in teas or in essential oil to help soothe sleep disturbances.

Nutritional Information

apple

An apple a day keeps the doctor away, right? Not only are apples known for their anticancerous properties and prevention of cardiovascular disease, they also help with respiratory problems, most notably asthma. And don't forget apples are very high in vitamin C, contributing to bone and teeth health, protecting against infection, and assisting in iron absorption (iron deficiency anemia most commonly affects babies nine to twenty-four months old).

apricot

This tiny fruit is one of the richest in provitamin A, minerals, and trace elements. Two apricots alone supply half the daily requirement of carotene, a cancer-fighting antioxidant. Apricots also provide a large amount of potassium, known for stimulating the elimination of toxins and for its healing properties, which is ideal for active children. Let's not forget the apricot's important contribution of iron, essential for little ones' development.

avocado

Extremely satiating and rich in fiber, avocados can have a positive effect on lazy bowels. Recent studies show the benefits of this fruit in treating liver problems. They're an equally excellent source of vitamins B5 (nerve impulses) and B6 (immune system).

banana

The banana is the champion of active babies: It's a very energizing fruit (90 calories for 3.5 ounces/100 g). It's important to note that the composition of this delectable fruit varies according to its maturity level. The riper the fruit, the less rich it is in vitamin C and starch, and the more simple sugars it contains. Bananas are also chock-full of potassium, iron, copper, calcium, magnesium, and vitamin B.

basil

The ancient Greeks lauded the virtues of basil—*basilikon* means "royal herb"—for its numerous health qualities. In fact, basil has antispasmodic and digestive properties that provide convincing results in the treatment of indigestion and heartburn. It's also a good source of vitamins A, B9, C, phosphorous, and calcium.

beef

Beef is a primary source for nutritional iron because it contains heme-iron, an iron that absorbs five times better than iron found elsewhere. Don't forget that growing children have a strong need for iron. Add to this that beef is an excellent source of ultra-high-quality protein, and thus B-group vitamins. Remember, though, not to overdo it, because in large doses beef can be detrimental to the cardiovascular system, due to the presence of saturated fatty acids.

bell pepper

Cousins to hot peppers (but without the spice), bell peppers are the fresh vegetable with the most vitamin C. It was actually in the bell pepper that A. Szent-Györgyi, a Hungarian scientist, first discovered vitamin C in the 1930s. Bell peppers are an excellent source of carotene and vitamin E, antioxidants known for preventing cancer and cardiovascular disease.

blueberry

This berry, very high in vitamin C (an antioxidant), has a protective and beneficial effect on vision. It is also said that blueberries have a beneficial effect on memory. Add to this the fact that blueberries are rich in potassium and phosphorous.

broccoli

This is a powerhouse of vitamin C: It contains twice the amount that an orange contains. In a 7-ounce (200 g) portion, you get more than your recommended daily requirement. Broccoli is equally very rich in provitamins, known for their antioxidant properties. Plus, broccoli has very few calories.

carrot

Bugs Bunny, who ate carrots to better keep an eye out for Elmer Fudd, knows it well—this orange root is rich in vitamin A, for fortifying the retina and improving night vision. But the virtues of this royal vegetable don't stop there. Packed with iron, it has powerful antianemic and antidiarrheal properties. Rich in carotene, substantial carrot consumption also provides nourishment for the skin.

cauliflower

Of all the vegetables, cauliflower boasts one of the highest concentrations of minerals, notably magnesium and calcium, which are essential for cellular renewal, and potassium, which stimulates renal function. With few calories, it is also very rich in vitamin C: A 7-ounce (200 g) portion covers the daily recommended amount.

celery root/celeriac

Very rich in minerals, this root vegetable also contains trace elements rarely found in other vegetables: most notably selenium (immune booster) and chromium (which facilitates assimilation of sugars). It is also loaded with fiber and low in calories.

cherry

Juicy and very sweet, the cherry is a refreshing energy fruit. In addition to contributing a big dose of vitamin C and provitamin A, it possesses good digestive properties.

chestnut

Chestnuts, considered a starch, are nevertheless high in vitamins and minerals. A 7.5-ounce (200 g) portion of cooked and mashed chestnuts meets 25 percent of the daily recommended allowance of magnesium (a relaxant). But the real benefit lies in the fact that chestnuts don't contain gluten, an ideal food for babies and children who have a gluten intolerance.

cilantro/coriander

Sometimes called "Chinese parsley," cilantro has been used since antiquity for its digestive and carminative (antibloating/flatulence) virtues. Used as an herbal infusion, cilantro is antidiarrheal and antispasmodic. Add to this its unique flavor and its important

contribution of vitamin K (which aids in blood clotting and bone formation), and you understand why Eastern peoples honor it so.

cod

This white fish has exceptional nutritional value. It's low in lipids and carbohydrates and rich in omega-3, vitamin B, selenium (antiradical), and phosphorous (bones and teeth). Let's not forget that cod offers plenty of iodine, a trace element that regulates the thyroid gland, which is responsible for calorie combustion.

corn

Rarely used in baby food (unfortunately), corn is a super grain, low in lipids but high in protein, fiber, B vitamins (for growth), and phosphorous (for bones and teeth). It also packs a powerful antioxidant punch.

cucumber

High in water content, cucumbers are swimming in minerals and trace elements like potassium, phosphorous, and calcium. They also provide vitamin B as well as vitamin A, necessary for healthy skin. Contrary to popular belief, cucumbers are easily digested and sit well in young bellies.

cumin

In addition to their robust flavor, these little seeds are a repository of benefits for babies. They stimulate digestion and, even more, decrease bloating and gas while calming intestinal spasms. Tack on to all this the fact that cumin also promotes lactation—a dream seed

for breast-feeding moms.

eggplant

With few calories and plenty of water, eggplants are equally rich in soft fibers called pectins, which gently aid digestion. If you find the laxative qualities in eggplants too strong, simply remove the seeds and skin. Don't forget that eggplants are rich in minerals (magnesium, zinc, and manganese) with minimal levels of sodium—perfect for baby meals.

fava bean

Low in calories, fresh fava beans have important nutritional qualities since they're essentially made of unsaturated fatty acids (cholesterol-fighting agents). They're also high in fiber (a powerful laxative) and contain a good amount of potassium, magnesium, and B and C vitamins. On top of all this, they're rich in protein and therefore perfect for those who don't eat meat and are seeking alternate sources of this dietary component.

fennel

A good source of antioxidant vitamins (A and E), fennel is rich in soft fiber, which helps to activate the bowel and facilitates movement through the intestine. It also has antibloating properties that are ideal in cases of excess gas. And don't forget that unique anise-like flavor!

garlic

Not only does garlic enhance all kinds of dishes, its medicinal properties are unequalled: It combats hypertension and reduces cholesterol levels, reinforces immune defenses, and has antiradical properties. It's also a mine of trace elements like iron, manganese, zinc, and selenium. Add to this antibacterial, antiallergenic, and anti-tumor abilities.

grapes

No need to argue the well-known benefits of grapes. Very energizing and nutritious, grapes nevertheless remain extremely digestible, perfect for a baby's immature digestive tract. In addition, grapes are detoxifiers, and they stimulate the liver. High in vitamins A, B, and C, they also contain magnesium, potassium, and a substantial amount of iron.

green beans

Green beans contain vitamins, minerals, and trace elements. Rich in provitamin A (which is good for growth and the immune system), as well as vitamins B (which stimulates appetite), C (which is good for healing and is antianemic), and E (which is antiradical). Green beans are also packed with potassium, calcium, iron, and protein.

lamb

Lamb is a rather fatty meat—the lipid content varies according to the cut of the animal—but its rich flavor and good proteins largely compensate for this small inconvenience. Lamb is also rich in vitamin B12, which is antianemic, and zinc, which is good for the heart and bones.

lemon

Sealed inside their thick rinds, lemons are champions of vitamin C. Heavy

on benefits, lemons are packed with potassium (a diuretic), calcium (for bones), and iron (for energy). They pair well with both savory and sweet in the kitchen.

lentils

A super legume, lentils are low in calories and have an incredible capacity to satiate without adding fat. They contain a record amount of minerals—much-needed iron being one of them. Rich in fiber, they are also good for combating constipation. Lentils contain a significant amount of vegetable protein (they rival meat protein when eaten with whole grains), and you can understand why cooks serve them so often.

mango

The mango is teeming with vitamins—of all fruits, it contains the most antioxidants (a half a mango covers all daily requirements). It has high amounts of vitamin B (for growth), vitamin A (for bones, teeth, and anti-infectant properties), vitamin C (for iron absorption), and vitamin E (for the immune system). Also worth boasting about is this fruit's 80 percent water content and its low calorie count.

melon

Though low in calories (they're 90 percent water), melons are not light on benefits, thanks to their treasure trove of provitamin A (especially true of orange melons like cantaloupes) and vitamin C. High in fiber, they can be mildly laxative, especially when eaten cold.

mint

In addition to its antioxidant properties, mint is rich in iron, manganese (when it's dried), and vitamin K (good for blood clotting). Not to mention its lovely refreshing taste.

muesli

Muesli (from Swiss German *müesli*) is a blend of various cereals, grains, and dried fruits according to taste. It's most often made of oats, wheat, rye, and barley flakes, and raisins, sometimes with walnuts, hazelnuts, flaxseed, pecans, or dried figs, depending on the season. The richness of the whole grains in muesli forms an incomparable source of fiber, proteins, and energy. For babies, choose a type of muesli that is gluten-free and does not have added sugar (you can always add honey or a lighter amount of sugar yourself).

nectarine

From the same family as the peach, nectarines boast many trace elements: phosphorous for the formation of bones, copper for tissue repair, and iron for the formation of cells. Nectarines are rich in vitamins B3 (good for energy production), C (a powerful antioxidant), and E (useful for cell protection).

oats

This super grain is rich in soluble fibers, whose effect on digestion and elimination is well known. Oats also have favorable effects on the regulation of cholesterol and blood sugar levels. They're rich in proteins and mono- and polyunsaturated fatty acids (the famous "good fats"). In addition, oats are loaded with iron, phosphorous, and magnesium, and are rich in vitamin B.

orange

Here's another vitamin C champion: One orange nearly covers the daily recommended allowance. Oranges contain a significant amount of soft fibers (ideal for difficult bowels), minerals, and trace elements.

parsnip

This elongated fleshy root that looks like a big white carrot (the two have common origins) has impressive nutritional qualities. Along with its slight hazelnut flavor, the parsnip boasts complex sugars and fructose, which calm hunger quickly with a lasting effect. It's also high in potassium (good for neuromuscular function and useful as an anti-stress agent), vitamin C, and folic acid (good for cell development and the nervous system).

pasta

Contrary to popular belief, pasta doesn't cause weight gain: Its lipid content is extremely low. It's the accompaniments we eat with pasta that pile on the calories. Made from wheat, pasta contains complex sugars that gradually release their energy. Perfect for mini-explorers on the go.

peach

Loaded with the antioxidants vitamin C and beta-carotene, peaches are your skin's best friends. They have a high water content and very little sugar, making them ideal summer snacks. The soft fibers in peaches are particularly

good for baby's fragile intestines and aid with constipation, especially when eaten raw. Plus, the alkalinity in peaches counteracts acidic foods.

pear

The soluble fibers in pears help with digestion. Pears have a high mineral content and contain significant amounts of calcium, phosphorous, magnesium, and iron. They are also loaded with vitamins C and E, and boast uncontested antioxidant virtues.

peas, sweet/green

Sweet peas are like beans: packed with energy and perfect for mini-athletes. Their protein and vitamin B (great for the immune system and for cell formation) content is almost five times greater than other fresh vegetables. Peas also happen to be full of minerals such as potassium and phosphorous, as well as trace elements (copper, zinc, and fluoride).

pineapple

Rich in minerals and trace elements, pineapples have a high vitamin C content despite their moderate calorie count. But the pineapple's major benefit is the presence of bromelain, an original enzyme that has the capacity to activate and facilitate the digestion of proteins.

plum

Their sweetness depends on the variety and the plum's maturity, but all plums are high in vitamins B and E and provitamin A, which is involved in cell growth and protection.

The fruit compensates for its low vitamin C content with the presence of pigments, which considerably reinforce the power of vitamin C. Plums are also high in potassium, calcium, magnesium, and several trace elements. Rich in soluble and insoluble fiber, plums aid with digestion and gently combat slow bowels.

yellow (mirabelle) plums

Found at produce stands from July through September, Mirabelle plums are little and yellow, juicy, sweet, and deliciously perfumed. They are very rich in trace elements and vitamins B and E.

pumpkin

Almost 90 percent water, pumpkins have few calories. Their ample potassium content helps prevent kidney stones as well as hypertension. Low in sodium, they're good for feeding Bébé, who can't withstand a heavy salt intake. Like carrots, pumpkins are well endowed with vitamin A—one portion of pumpkin covers the daily recommended allowance for an adult.

raspberry

Low in calories and slightly acidic, raspberries are the perfect summer dessert. High in fiber, they can have laxative effects. Sensitive tummies prefer them puréed into a fruit coulis and strained of their seeds. Raspberries offer many minerals, including potassium, magnesium, calcium, and iron. They're also rich in vitamin C and flavonoids (which are helpful to blood circulation).

rice

After wheat, rice is the most consumed grain in the world. Very satisfying, it's also prized for its nutritional value. It's rich in magnesium and contains phosphorous, zinc, vitamin B, and potassium. Rice has antidiarrheal effects—especially its cooking water—and it has a positive effect on hypertension.

rutabaga

The rutabaga is a cross between the cabbage and the turnip. It's rich in potassium, calcium, phosphorous, and vitamin C. In addition, rutabaga is low in calories. It's also been ascribed digestive virtues and is a reputed intestinal disinfectant.

saffron

Saffron has long been known to remedy ailments. The pigment responsible for its deep red-orange color also stimulates digestion. Saffron also has analgesic and sedative qualities, perfect for troubled sleep or anxiety. North African folk remedies for teething pains are made from honey and saffron.

sage

Known as the "marvelous plant" by the ancient Gauls of France, sage possesses incomparable anti-inflammatory powers, wound-healing abilities, and tonic, digestive, and antiseptic properties, too. Sage is also high in vitamin K, which helps with blood clotting.

salmon

Whether wild or farmed, salmon has exceptional nutritional virtues. It's a fatty ("good fat") fish that's extremely rich in omega-3, one of the essentials for cardiovascular health. Salmon contributes an ample amount of iron, phosphorous, and magnesium as well as a significant amount of vitamins A (for vision, growth, and immune defenses) and D (for teeth and bones).

strawberry

Besides its one-of-a-kind flavor, which happens to be the favorite of children everywhere, the strawberry is packed with folic acid (beneficial for cell renewal), beta-carotene (helpful for the immune system) and vitamin C (useful as an antioxidant). It's also rich in trace elements like potassium (valuable for the nervous system), magnesium (helpful as a relaxant), and calcium (necessary for bone health). However, your doctor may recommend waiting until your baby gourmet is over twelve months old before introducing strawberries, as they can cause allergic reactions.

sweet potato

Originally from South America before growers cultivated them in the Caribbean, sweet potatoes resemble regular potatoes in many culinary ways (however, with the addition of an undoubtable sweetness). And they clearly stand apart when compared nutritionally. Sweet potatoes possess a very low rating on the glycemic index and offer a consequential contribution in vitamin A—a skin protector, a powerful anti-infectant, and an immune-system booster.

tarragon

An herb known for its full-bodied, hint-of-licorice flavor, tarragon is an appetite stimulant with digestive and antibloating properties. It's also abundant in minerals and vitamin C, making it a powerful detoxification agent that's ideal for urban environments.

thyme

Thyme is a real multipurpose medicine. It stimulates the appetite and guards against bloating while offering antibacterial and even antiseptic properties. Use it as an herbal infusion to treat minor colds.

tomato

With a very high water content (95 percent), tomatoes are low in calories and an excellent source of minerals (perfect for remineralizing an overheated body). They're full of potassium (good for combating hypertension), magnesium, zinc, phosphorous, and iron. Tomatoes are also an excellent source of vitamins A, B, and C. Perhaps their best asset is their gorgeous red color, which comes from the lycopene they contain. In humans, this precious pigment protects cells from free radical attack and plays an important role as an antioxidant and preventer of some kinds of cancer.

vanilla

Besides its wonderfully sweet flavor, vanilla possesses sedative qualities and is sometimes used as an herbal infusion or with aromatherapy to calm troubled sleep. A recent study conducted at the Hospital of Strasbourg and led by Luc Marlier (of the French National Center for Scientific Research) demonstrated that premature babies exposed to the scent of vanilla had more regular breathing patterns and were 45 percent less likely to experience sleep apnea. The scent of vanilla enticed babies to suckle, nurse, and relax. Use it to prepare for a good night's sleep!

zucchini

Though low in calories, zucchini is extremely high in minerals and vitamins such as A (beneficial to bones and teeth, and an anti-infective), B (good for general growth and the immune system), and C (useful for healing and iron absorption). When eaten young, it contains particularly tender fibers, well suited for fragile digestive systems. The perfect vegetable for *les petits*!

Acknowledgments

I am truly proud of this personal recipe book, which was—until now—just a workbook, written by hand, worn out, and full of stains. Today that workbook has become this book thanks to the many people who put up with me: testers, supporters, sources of inspiration, editors, and so on.

Huge thanks first of all to Marabout, to Emmanuel and Amaryllis, who gave me the opportunity to write this book and who believed in me. Thanks to them, this book is really beautiful, personal, and original. Thanks also to Fred and Sonia Lucano for the magnificent photographs and to the baby models who really got into the spirit. And a giant *merci* to Cédrine Meier—who, thanks to her formidable talent for writing, helped me make the text readable, relevant, and funny.

Great thanks, as well, to my friend Dr. Jean Lalau Keraly, who has supported me from the very first day, who is always on hand with advice, and who is extremely generous with his time.

Thank you to The Experiment for allowing this book to reach its North American audience, including my American editor Cara Bedick, managing editor Karen Giangreco, publisher Matthew Lore, and everyone else who pitched in on this edition. It also wouldn't have been possible without the translation skills of Christine Buckley.

I also want to pay homage to my husband, David, who through his support, tolerance, and involvement in our family allowed me to throw myself into the crazy adventure that is Baby Meals (Les Menus Bébé), as well as work day and night on this book.

Finally, the biggest thanks of all to my children, Maya and Milo. You are my reason for living and my inspiration. All of this is thanks to you. I love you like crazy!

Thanks to White and Brown household appliances.

All the babies in this book were dressed by Lily & the Funky Boys. Thanks, Esther!

	4 months+	6 months+	9 months+	12 months+
APPLE	26, 34	55, 66		126, 160, 165
APRICOT	28	52	86	107
AVOCADO	41			124
BANANA	32			146, 151, 156, 160
BEEF		59		108, 109
BELL PEPPER				128, 134, 138, 142
BLUEBERRY		70		
BROCCOLI	38	53, 58		
BUTTERNUT SQUASH			83	
CARROT	36	52, 56, 59, 63, 67	82, 86	104, 106, 107, 109, 122, 124, 136
CAULIFLOWER	44			
CELERY ROOT		57, 58		126
CHERRY	34	70		
CHERRY TOMATOES				116, 125, 128, 133, 134
CLEMENTINE		74		151
COCONUT MILK				104, 136, 142
CORN	46	54	99	124, 138
EGGPLANT		64	86, 87	
FAVA BEANS		62	93	118, 125
FENNEL		56, 57, 63		
FIG				161
FISH		60, 61, 62, 63, 64		110, 116, 118, 120
GINGER		55	86	104, 106, 136, 142
GREEN BEANS	40	53, 58	90	104, 120, 138
GREEN GRAPES		63		151
GREEN LENTILS			94	
HAM				112, 114
HONEY				140, 146, 148, 149, 156, 161
LAMB		58		107
LYCHEE	33			160
MANGO	32	73, 74		146, 151, 156, 160
MELON	29	74		150
MILK CHOCOLATE				164
MINT		72		149
MUESLI				146, 148, 149
NECTARINE		73		

	4 months+	6 months+	9 months+	12 months+
ONION		54		108
ORANGE		74		116
ORANGE JUICE	36	52, 56, 63	84	106, 122
PARMESAN		69	80	113, 125, 128, 132, 135
PARSNIP	43	57, 63		126
PASTA			88	112, 130, 132, 133, 134, 135
PEACH	24	74		150, 156
PEAR	27, 35			161
PEAS	39	58	90	112, 114, 120, 130, 135, 138, 140
PEPPER				108, 109
PINEAPPLE	33			
PLUM	35			
POTATO	45, 46	60, 66, 68		108, 120
POULTRY		52, 53, 54, 55		104, 106, 113, 114
PUMPKIN	45	66	96	142
PRUNE				164
RAISINS		63		106, 146, 154, 164
RASPBERRY		72		149, 150, 156, 162, 166
RED LENTIL				122, 136
RICE			80	113, 138, 142
RUTABAGA		57		126
SEMOLINA		69	84	110
SOFT CHEESE			88, 98	
SPINACH		61	92, 94	
STRAWBERRY		72		150, 156, 162, 165
SUGAR SNAP PEAS				135
SWEET POTATO	42	60	96	114, 142
TOMATO		59, 64	82, 86, 87, 91, 99	106, 107, 108, 109, 126, 128, 136
TURNIP		53, 58, 68		
VANILLA BEAN				96, 152, 153, 161, 162
VEAL		56, 57		
WATERMELON		74		
WHOLE GRAIN BREAD				158, 160, 161
YELLOW PLUM	30			148
YOGURT		70		122, 152, 156
ZUCCHINI		53, 58, 59, 62, 64	86, 87, 90, 93	104, 106, 107, 109, 122

Index

The numbers in parentheses indicate the age (in months) for which a recipe is suitable.